PERSONAL COMPUTING

PERSONAL COMPUTING

A Beginner's Guide

David Bunnell

HAWTHORN BOOKS, INC.
Publishers/NEW YORK
A Howard & Wyndham Company

Dedicated to the people who stood
by me, sometimes having more
faith in what I was doing
than I did:
especially

Kim Behm
Linda Essay Bunnell
Dick Brown
Austin Cragg
Ed Currie
Don Nace
George Palken
Ed Roberts
Nels Winkless
and my dad and mom, Hugh and Elois

I asked the computer,
"Is there a God?"
And the computer replied,
"ERROR 02 SYNTAX."

CONTENTS

PERSONAL COMPUTING

INTRODUCTION:
THE REVOLUTION BEGINS

The scene is the beautiful but dusty little city of Albuquerque, New Mexico. A small electronics company, unnoticed by most people except for the handful of creditors who haven't received a check for several months, is quietly working on a project that will have an impact on society literally as revolutionary as the printing press or the steam engine or the automobile. It is the fall of 1974, and unless the project is completed soon, the little company will simply disappear and no one will hear about its dream. The company president, Ed Roberts, has mortgaged his house and stands to lose everything. He's been working day and night, drinking too much coffee and smoking too many cigarettes. His smoker's hack is so bad that he frequently has to cover the mouthpiece on his telephone when receiving calls.

The little company, which only a few months earlier consisted of 85 employees including engineers, production workers, technicians, technical writers, bookkeepers, etc., is now down to fewer than 20 people, most of whom are working for reduced salaries and looking around for something else in case this project, a kit computer, known internally as "Roberts's folly," doesn't get out the door before the bank closes the door permanently.

Roberts schedules a plane trip to New York where he will meet with the editors of *Popular Electronics* magazine to try to convince them to put the computer on the cover of their January 1975 issue. A prototype of the computer, which as yet does not even have a name, is shipped ahead of time via air freight. It should be there when Roberts arrives.

Roberts arrives in New York and, as Murphy's Law would dictate, the computer has been lost by the air freight company. He nervously places a call to his chief engineer and longtime friend, Bill Yates, who frantically begins building a second prototype. Armed with schematic diagrams, desperation, and a lot of guts, Roberts heads for the offices of *Popular Electronics* where he will try to show the editors what his computer could do if they only had one.

Fortunately for Roberts and for the revolution, one of the editors, Les Solomon, takes a personal interest in the computer, even going so far as to come up with a name for it, Altair.* Solomon has worked with Roberts in the past on calculator projects, and he knows that Ed is a man of his word even if he is working with limited resources. He actually believes that a prototype exists and that Roberts will have another one delivered to *Popular Electronics* in a couple of weeks if the lost version is not recovered. Even more incredible is the fact that Solomon believes the computer will really work.

In January 1975 the revolution begins. The Altair, which sells as a kit for under $400 and has the same computing capabilities of $20,000- to $50,000-computers, is featured on the cover of *Popular Electronics*. Expecting to sell 400 computers the first year (enough to pay off the bank debt), the little company is overwhelmed by more than 1500 orders, cash in advance, by the end of February. Roberts, who knows no limits to his entrepreneurial ambitions, takes out a full-page ad in *Scientific American* and begins talking about the demise of IBM.

*Solomon received this suggestion from his 16-year-old daughter who had been watching "Star Trek." The Enterprise was going to visit a planet in the Altair system. Altair is one of the brighter stars in the heavens as seen from Earth.

The little company starts down the harried road to becoming a bigger company, runs into a huge roadblock called cash flow, and sells out to a big computer company in California, but not before *Business Week* refers to it as the "IBM of the microcomputer industry." And not before it has developed a whole new market for computers.

At first, there were the computer hobbyists (sometimes referred to as computer freaks). They were experimenters who liked building computers from kits, testing them with their own oscilloscopes, carefully examining each and every part, in many cases developing better computer equipment of their own, and inventing new and marvelous ways to use this amazing tool. Then there were forward-looking people who wanted to use computers in their business and professional lives. There were pharmacists who found they could use computers to speed the time required to fill prescriptions by letting the computer handle the bookwork and print the labels. Small retailers found they could keep both better track of their inventories and more accurate, up-to-date books. Teachers discovered that they could use the computer as an instruction aid and as a method of cutting down the time needed for grading papers and keeping records. People started using computers in their homes, first as a source of entertainment, with complicated computer games, then as recipe files, and as record-keeping, check balancing, and budgeting aids. They began to hook up their computers to other devices, such as their lighting and heating systems, their stereos and alarm clocks. They began to communicate with other home computer users through telephone hookups and with large computer information libraries. And this was only the beginning.

The little company that started it all was named Mits, and I was one of its 20 employees, in charge of technical writing and advertising. I've grown with this revolution and tried to help it along wherever I could. It has been my role to attempt to explain to outsiders what the hell is going on.

At the time of this writing there were about 100,000 individuals using computers in the United States. In the short time since the idea caught on, over 1000 computer retail stores have sprung up across the country. Personal computing shows held in most major cities have drawn over 250,000 stupefied attendants. And personal computers are being produced by 50 different companies, including Radio Shack, Heath, Montgomery Ward, APF, and Commodore.

The reason for the fantastic growth of this industry in just three years is simple: *The personal computer represents increased personal power.* It gives us the ability to fight back, to cope with the complications of our increasing bureaucratic, paper-ridden society. It is an equalizer in the new world of technology.

For as little as $400 you can buy a computer today and put it to use realizing your own intellectual, aesthetic, and economic potentials. "Power to the people" is perhaps a more fitting slogan when applied to today's personal computer than it was when it was applied to the social movements of the 1960s. Think how potent a weapon the computer can be for the middle-class citizen fed up with soaring taxes, dishonest politicians, inadequate schools, government interference, utility companies, oil companies, mass congestion, and runaway inflation.

After reading this book you will, hopefully, understand computers and how to get started with them; and I hope you will see the vision. The full impact of the personal computer will become more apparent as the technology becomes more refined and as more people discover it. Still, momentous breakthroughs have been achieved, and like it or not, the age of the personal computer is upon us.

1

HOW IT WORKS:
A NOT SO RIDICULOUS,
RIDICULOUS EXAMPLE

It is time to shatter a few myths about computers. The most prevalent myth is that computers are very large, complicated machines that can only be operated by highly intelligent men in little white jackets. This myth was once a reality because many large computer companies, especially IBM, wanted it that way. As long as computers could only be understood and operated by the people that made them, computer companies could pretty much have their way as to how computers were used, thus ensuring their own prosperity. IBM prospered to the extent that one of its current corporate problems is how to spend the excess billions in cash it has in various bank accounts.

The myths about computers scare many people—and with good reason. If only a few men in white jackets can use computers and if computers are going to control much of what goes on in our world, then those few men can become very powerful. Science fiction is full of examples of computers taking over the world and running it as if ordinary people were the expendable machines. What is most frightening, though, is that these possibilities were never really farfetched.

One of the major problems that marketers of personal computers are up against is this fear. People are afraid to

Computers are no longer large, complicated machines that can only be operated by highly intelligent men in little white jackets. These two children are using a VideoBrain computer to practice arithmetic drills. (*Courtesy VideoBrain Computer Company*)

touch a computer. They are afraid they can't possibly understand how to use one. The computer intimidates them.

Back in the 1890s, when the government first put the Plains Indians on reservations, it was decided that each Indian family would be equipped with a wagon and a couple of horses. These Indians needed horses and wagons in order to learn how to be farmers, but most of them were afraid of wagons, and instead of riding in them, they walked along beside them. The story with today's computers is much the same. We can't afford to walk along beside the computer and let other people control it. We must climb aboard now and take control of our own destinies.

So before we do anything else, it is appropriate that we sit down at a computer and try it. Imagine the following:

A TV screen

A cassette tape recorder

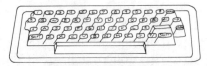

A typewriter keyboard

The TV screen is exactly like the TV screen in your house, except that it doesn't have a channel selector. Instead, it has a little red button. Push this button and the TV screen will light up.

The typewriter keyboard is exactly like the typewriter keyboard on your typewriter, except that it has a few extra keys. For this example we need only be concerned about the large key on the right labeled ENTER. There is a red button on the back of this keyboard. Push it and the computer, which is cleverly hidden inside the keyboard case, will turn on. Now look at the screen. It says READY.

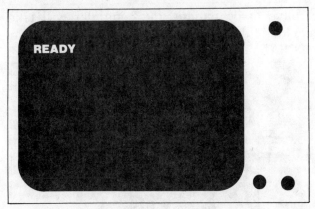

READY

The cassette recorder is exactly like cassette recorders you've used in the past except that the microphone is missing (you don't need it). Next to the cassette recorder is a cassette tape labeled BLACKJACK. Pick it up and put it into the tape recorder. Press the PLAY button on the recorder. Nothing happens, but don't worry about it. The recorder is not broken.

Now, here's the hard part. Turn once again to the keyboard and type the word *CLOAD*, making sure you don't leave a space between C and LOAD. (CLOAD stands for cassette load. It is used when loading a program from a cassette tape to the computer.) Come on now, you've used a typewriter many times and this is no different. That's it, now press the ENTER key we talked about. Bingo, the cassette recorder, which didn't start running when you first pressed the PLAY button, is now running. A little blinking star appears on the screen above the word *READY*. This tells you that the computer program BLACKJACK is being loaded into the computer.

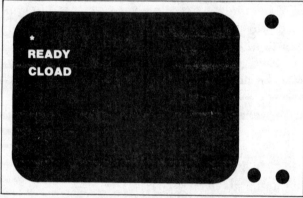

You have to be patient, the computer will take a few minutes to load this program. Once it is loaded, the screen will again say READY.

So far, so good. Now, return to the keyboard and type the word *RUN* (which means "start the program"), and then once again press the ENTER key. Wow, look what happens; the screen goes blank, and then:

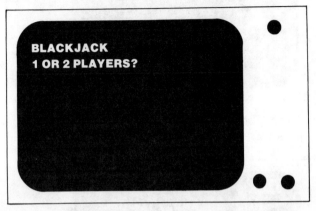

The computer is asking you a question! Go ahead, answer it, *always remembering to follow your answer by pressing the ENTER key,* which actually enters information into the computer. Assuming your answer is 1, the screen will now look like this:

For the sake of the example, let's say your name is Jack. You answer JACK, press the ENTER key, the screen goes blank, and then:

Now don't be chicken, this isn't for real. Go ahead, bet $500. Enter $500 and press the ENTER key. Look at that:

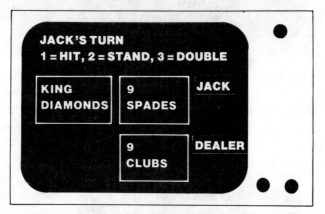

You've drawn a 9 and a king for a total of 19. The dealer has a 9 showing. Unless there's an ace under the hidden card, you're bound to at least tie. The smart thing to do is press 2 (indicating that you choose to stand pat) and then ENTER. Look at that: the dealer had an 8 and you've won $500. Now the screen looks like this:

See how easy that was? Now, suppose you have a computer like this and you have thousands of cassette tapes to choose from. Besides playing blackjack, checkers, backgammon, and many other games, you have programs on cassette tape for balancing your checkbook, keeping track of inventory, figuring your income taxes, storing addresses and phone numbers, etc. Not only can you immediately start doing these things, but once you learn a few simple tricks with the computer, you'll be writing your own programs.

A computer like the one used in this example is available today from Radio Shack for less than $600. If this sounds interesting to you, read on. We've only just begun!

2

COMPUTER APPLICATIONS

The example shown in chapter 1 should give you a taste of what computers do, but of course there is a lot more to them than playing blackjack. It is not true, as some of the more boisterous computer enthusiasts claim, that you can use a personal computer to do *anything* you want it to do. As the sophistication of these machines increases and as more innovative people put them to work, it is likely that some really astonishing uses (or to use the computer term, *applications*) will be found. Before you buy a computer, though, you should be aware of some of its real limitations. For instance, don't expect your computer to play championship chess. There are large computers capable of playing a very sophisticated game of chess, but, as of this writing, no one has trained a personal computer to play anything but a slow, plodding game that any amateur player can beat. And don't be disappointed if you can't store Webster's dictionary in your computer; the truth is, computer memory can be very expensive, and you'd have to enter the information in Webster's word by word, which could take a while.

Well then, what can you do with your own computer? Here are some examples of what some people are already doing.

Budgeting

This is an application that could easily make the computer pay for itself. The advantages of doing your household budget via computer are twofold: (1) The computer will automatically do all the calculations, such as finding the percentage of your income you spent last month on entertainment; and (2) because of the interactive characteristics of the computer, it will prompt you to answer the correct questions, such as "DID YOU SPEND ANY MONEY TODAY ON GASOLINE?"

At the end of each month the computer will print out or display a monthly summary of your spending habits. Just keeping track of these things can teach you how to cut down on the areas where you are being wasteful. How many people can tell how much money they spent last month on food, clothing, eating out, movies, etc.? Keeping track of expenses is the first step to spending your income more efficiently. And look at the bright side: you may find out that you are better off than you think.

Writing Letters

Suppose you are secretary of the local Lions Club and your organization has just completed a very successful fund-raising effort to build a new teen center in your community. You want to write a letter to all the contributors thanking them for their support.

The trouble is, you are a very busy person and the time required to write 150 individual letters is a real killer. At 10 minutes a letter, it will take you 25 hours to complete this task. With the right computer system you could write to each contributor by name, thanking him or her personally and even mentioning the amount of money they contributed.

All you have to do is write the text of the letter, which can be stored in the computer's memory, and instruct the computer to enter the person's name and the amount of the contribution in selected places.

Clever grammar in the text will avoid inconsistencies in the tense of a verb or with plurals, and the computer will automatically make adjustments for the length of names or copy you want inserted to avoid unsightly gaps or crowding.

Storing Addresses

With the same computer you use to write thank-you letters to the contributors of your fund-raising event, you could also store the names and addresses of the contributors. These addresses could be printed out by the computer on gummed labels to cut back drastically the time required for addressing envelopes.

Suppose you have 10,000 names and addresses stored on the computer instead of 150. These are names of people all over the country who might want to contribute to a national fund-raising campaign you're organizing.

Now then, besides the time-saving features of the computer in this situation, the computer could also cut your postage bill almost in half. This is because the post office has a special rate (called a bulk rate) for organizations that do a lot of mailing which at the time of this writing was 7.5 cents per piece instead of 13 cents. However, in order to qualify for this rate, you must organize your mail in bundles according to zip code order. The rate is justified because you do much of the work that the post office has to do for first-class mail.

The computer could be instructed to print out the 10,000 labels in zip code order so that you could accomplish this sorting process without any difficulty at all. Or say you only wanted to mail to people on your list that live in a five-state area. The computer could be instructed just to print out these addresses. Or it could be instructed to print out the names in alphabetical order.

Large companies, magazines, and political organizations, just to name a few, have relied on the computer for years to handle their mailing lists. Just imagine the power a personal computer could give you if you used it just to handle this one task.

One word of caution here: The $600 computer we mentioned will not handle mailing lists without the addition of some relatively expensive equipment. In order for the computer to print anything, you'll need to have it hooked up to a special computer typewriter called a line printer. These printers can cost anywhere from $500 to $5000 depending upon size, speed and sophistication. Also, to handle a large list of addresses and have the ability to manipulate those addresses according to zip code or alphabetical order, you'll need a better memory storage device than a simple cassette recorder. What you'll need is a device called a disk storage unit, which is simply a box that hooks onto the computer and stores memory on disks that look very much like records. These disk systems are also priced from $500 and up. One final component in the computer system we are describing is the *software* or *computer program* that will tell the computer how to handle a given task. Once you become an expert, you'll be able to write your own programs, but for the time being, ready-made programs are best.

Just Plain Writing

As long as we are on the subject of what in the computer business is called *word processing,* we should take a look at the advantages of using the computer as a writing tool for tasks other than computerized letters.

Imagine that you are a famous or not-so-famous novelist and that you must return a manuscript to your publisher in three weeks or face the possibility of forfeiting the nice advance that they've promised you. Using a conventional typewriter, you confront an enormous task, for each time you revise a sentence or paragraph, you're going to have to retype a whole page or series of pages. Actually, the task of going from rough draft to first-final draft to final-final draft to revised draft to final-revised draft is what kills off a lot of writers. Creating the text of your book might come easy to you, but getting it down on paper in time for the deadline could be where you fall on your face.

With a computer, you could store the text of your manuscript in the computer's memory by writing on the TV screen with the computer's typewriter style keyboard much as we did with the blackjack example. You could call up the manuscript page by page and make corrections right on the screen without having to retype extraneous material. If you wanted to insert a paragraph, the computer would automatically insert it in the body of the text. If you wanted to make a spelling correction or rewrite a phrase or sentence, you could simply move the computer's *cursor* (the place on the screen where you are writing) to the proper position and enter your correction.

Connected to a line printer, such as the Sprint Micro 5 pictured here, your personal computer can become a powerful writing machine. (*Courtesy Qume Corporation*)

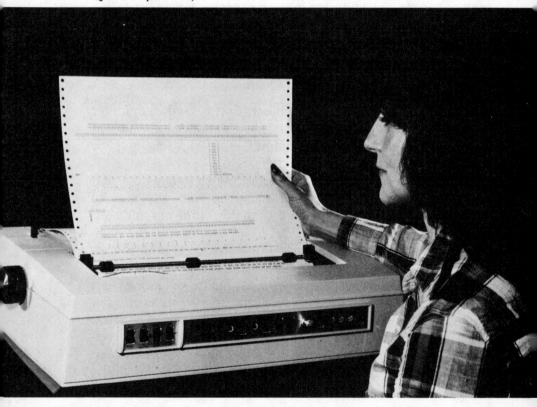

Once you have the manuscript completed, you simply instruct the computer to print it out on the line printer. The text is still stored in the computer's memory so that you can easily make any additional corrections anytime you want. There. You've just saved about a thousand hours of typing or a stiff fee to a typist.

Automatic Testing Machine

If you are a student or if you want to increase your knowledge of a specific subject, you can use the computer as an automatic testing machine. Simply put the information you wish to learn in the computer and instruct it to ask you questions. Let's say you want to be able to recall the capitals of all the states. The computer might ask you:

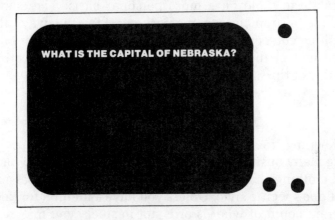

WHAT IS THE CAPITAL OF NEBRASKA?

If you answer "OMAHA" the computer might be programmed to say, "NO, DUMMY, THE CAPITAL OF NEBRASKA BEGINS WITH THE LETTER L." This clue, which is an option you have programmed into the computer, tells you that your answer is wrong and that the capital of Nebraska begins with the letter "L." Next, if you try "LARAMIE," the computer might respond with, "COME ON NOW, TRY AGAIN. THE FIRST TWO LETTERS IN THE CAPITAL OF NEBRASKA ARE LI." This time you answer correctly by entering "LINCOLN," and the computer responds with "THAT'S CORRECT. BUT IT TOOK YOU THREE TRIES." If, after several attempts, you can't remember the correct answer, the computer could be coded to give you the answer. Type the word "ANSWER" onto the screen. The computer might say, "THE CAPITAL OF NEBRASKA IS LINCOLN. JUST REMEMBER THAT IT'S NAMED AFTER A FAMOUS PRESIDENT OR THAT IT'S WHERE THE UNIVERSITY OF NEBRASKA FOOTBALL TEAM IS. NOW THEN, WHAT IS THE CAPITAL OF SOUTH DAKOTA?"

Communicating with a computer in this fashion, where it asks you a question and then immediately responds to your answer, is called *interactive computing*. The nice part of it is that no one needs to know that it took you three tries to figure out what the capital of Nebraska is. This example might sound ridiculous, but suppose you are a salesman and want to remember the names of all your potential clients so that you can relate to them on a more personal basis. The computer could be a tremendous memory aid. By the way, this is something you could do on a $600 computer. You don't need a line printer or disk system for this particular application, or for many of the following applications.

Inventory

Keeping track of inventory is one of the major problems facing many businesses today. Suppose you are the owner of a small clothing shop and you sell a whole stock of dresses that are of one specific style. Unless you have a method for keeping a current count of what is or is not in stock, you may not discover that this particular item is selling well until it is too late to order more. A good computerized inventory system could have alerted you to the fact that your supply was running out.

Inventory applications can be found in the home, also. Have you ever had the unfortunate experience of a burglary or fire? Just remembering what items you have in your house, how much they cost, and when you purchased them can be a real problem for both you and your insurance agent.

You could use a computer to store a list of all this information. Whenever you purchase something of value, such as a

Keeping track of inventory, payroll, general ledger accounting, accounts receivable, and accounts payable are just a few of the uses for a personal computer in business. (*Courtesy Radio Shack*)

new washing machine, you could update your list by adding the new item and deleting the old item, assuming you had an old washing machine in the first place.

Several people have suggested using the computer to keep a kitchen inventory of what food is on hand. Each week before you go to the grocery store, you ask the computer to print out or display a list of items that you are running short of. The problem with this kind of inventory program is that you would have to sit down at the computer daily and enter the amount of any food you used. Seems to me that this application would be too much trouble. However, suppose you decide to start a small restaurant. . . .

Diet Planning

If you want to plan meals for you or for your family in order to stay trim and healthy or because you have some special dietary requirements, you can use a computer to simplify this task.

One program already available lets you plan a menu for the whole month and then compares this menu to your kitchen inventory program. The computer will tell you when you are short of the raw ingredients. For instance, if you've planned on serving a cheese and broccoli casserole for Wednesday evening, the computer will alert you on Tuesday that you are short on cheese. Also, the computer can be instructed to give you automatically a calorie and nutrition content count on each meal you serve. If you haven't been getting the minimum daily requirement of protein, the computer can alert you to this fact.

Amortization

Let's say your rich aunt dies and you come into $20,000 or so. If you wanted to apply half of this amount to your house payments, how would this alter your equity situation? How long would it now take you to finish up paying for your house? These questions and others like them can be solved by a computer with an amortization program. These programs instruct the computer to print out or display the information concerning any loan and what your payments, equity situation, and interest will be if you decide to make more than one payment. Everyone borrows these days, so this would be a useful program to have around.

Check Balancing

Balancing your checkbook by computer can get to be a pain because you have to sit down at the keyboard and enter all the checks you write, the amount of each check, and the check numbers. Then when you get your bank statement, you have to enter this information to find out what checks are outstanding. It doesn't seem to me that the computer offers many advantages here over using a calculator and the balancing sheet in the back of your checkbook. Sure, the computer will automatically do the calculations, but you are faced with the problems of entering every check twice, first in the checkbook when you write the check, and then once again in the computer.

The advantage of using a computer for check balancing comes at income tax time. Every check you write during the year can be coded according to medical expense, house payment, car payment, food, utilities, etc. At the end of the year, the computer can be instructed to print out or display a list of all the checks you wrote that are tax deductible. Instead of spending hours digging through cancelled checks, you can instantly find out how many deductions you are entitled to. Also the computer could automatically figure out how much interest you have paid on your car and house payments. Just imagine the amount of money the average citizen loses each year because he or she doesn't have a method for keeping accurate spending records. Many people fill out the short form at income tax time when using the long form with itemized deductions could save them considerable amounts of money.

Recently, I saw a cartoon in a computer hobbyist magazine depicting a man with a pushcart on which there was a computer. The man was standing inside an IRS office. A clerk was giving him a rather awkward look, and the caption read, "Meet my accountant."

Income Tax Preparation

Unfortunately for the accounting business and the many firms that figure out the average citizen's income tax, the home computer will eventually take over this function. The advantage of using a computer to figure your taxes is that it's there when you are ready, much of the necessary information is already stored inside the computer, and it doesn't cost you anything. One more advantage is that unless you have a faulty income tax program in your computer, it will not make a mistake. My grandfather, who had less than an eighth grade education, was once fined over $200,000 by the government because his accountant made a mistake on his income taxes. If he had only had a personal computer, he might have been able to hang onto his ranch in Colorado, and today I'd be a rich cowboy hustling cattle instead of grinding out a living on a typewriter. There must be hundreds of similar stories.

Figuring Golf Handicaps

Do you realize that the average golf course calculates over 8000 handicaps per year and that each one requires at least 720 additions, subtractions, sorting routines, divisions, multiplications, and order listings? This means that the average golf course is burdened with approximately 12,000,000 calculations per year.

Gene Dial, who is an enterprising computer hobbyist, wrote an article entitled "Golfcap" for the August 1977 issue of *Personal Computing* magazine in which he explained how to set up a computer to solve this problem. While the instructions are a bit too lengthy to repeat here, suffice it to say that it can be done. If you're not a golfer, perhaps you're a bowler or a bridge player. Any recreational activity that requires a large number of calculations is an appropriate candidate for computer application.

Memory Aid

Did you forget to send your Aunt Mabel a card on her last birthday or have you ever had the unfortunate experience of forgetting your own wedding anniversary? If you can get yourself into the habit of sitting down at the computer every day or at least twice a week to do the programming, the computer can be taught to remind you of important dates and events.

Sales Analysis

If you are the manager of a retail business, you can use an inexpensive computer system to analyze your monthly sales.

The computer will show you each category of sales, the gross for the month, the amount of dollars per sale, the percentage this represents of your overall business, and so forth. Using this information, you can make intelligent decisions about which areas of your business you should concentrate on. For example, if you run a portrait studio, it may be that the majority of your sales are coming from photographing school children, but the time required for each sale is much greater in relation to the income received than the time required for photographing weddings. The intelligent thing for you to do in this situation is to advertise the wedding portrait aspect of your business. That way you can increase your gross revenue without increasing your work load.

Even if you are only interested in using a computer in your home, it is important for you to be aware of the business applications that a computer can provide. Almost everyone, someday in his life, decides that he would really like to go into business for himself. In the past, this has been a very difficult procedure. As a matter of fact, over 70 percent of all new business started each year go bankrupt. With personal computers, budding entrepreneurs will be able to manage their money and time, and they will have a much better chance of overcoming the complications of starting and maintaining a business.

Personal computers could very well revitalize the free enterprise system because small entrepreneurs will have the same access to data that large companies already have. This is certainly one of the revolutionary aspects of personal computing.

Making Decisions

Phil Feldman and Tom Rugg have created a computer program that will aid you in making almost any decision. Their program, along with an explanation of how to use it, was published in the July 1977 issue of *Kilobaud* magazine.

In the example presented by Feldman and Rugg, a man named Joe is trying to decide which automobile he should buy. He has narrowed his choice down to a Dodge Aspen, a Volvo, or a Chevrolet Nova. Just for fun, Joe throws in a Rolls Royce because it gives him a way to check the validity of the results. If the Rolls doesn't come out on the bottom of his list, he knows the program is faulty.

Joe decided that the factors that were important in making this decision were fuel economy, handling ease and comfort, aesthetics, maintenance, price, and safety. Price was the most important of these considerations, so he gave it a value of 10. The other values ranged from 4 for aesthetics to 9 for fuel economy. As you can see from this, Joe is a very practical person. Other people might be more concerned about appearances than fuel economy and price. Still others might have rated safety as the most important consideration.

Joe then had to come up with a value for each car in each of the categories. In each case he assigned the value 10 to the Dodge Aspen and then rated the other cars relative to this. A value higher than 10 meant that he considered that car to be better than the Aspen and a value lower meant that he considered it to be not as good as the Aspen.

Once all this information was entered into the computer, it calculated the overall results for each car on a scale from 1 to 100, taking into consideration the priority values Joe assigned to each category. In this particular case, the Chevy Nova was rated slightly better than the Dodge Aspen, with the Volvo a distant third, and the Rolls way out of the picture.

The interesting aspect of this use of a computer is that the computer makes its decision based on the individual's preferences. If safety and appearance were more important to Joe than price and fuel economy, the Rolls or the Volvo probably would have come out on top.

Recipe Storage

Have you ever come across the problem of wanting to serve an exotic dish to a party of nine but the recipe in your cookbook, which is long and complicated, serves only four people? One of the nice features of recipe storage on a computer is that the computer automatically tabulates the proper amount of ingredients for whatever number of people you want to serve.

With the proper computer system, the process of finding a particular recipe is much simpler than looking through recipe books. If you want Italian Spaghetti, you can simply type "ITALIAN SPAGHETTI" on your computer display and it might respond with: "WITH OR WITHOUT MEATBALLS?" You then enter "MEATBALLS" and the computer asks you "HOW MANY PEOPLE WILL YOU BE SERVING?" You enter "15" and, presto, a recipe for Italian Spaghetti with meatballs serving 15 people appears on the screen.

Speech Recognition

With the addition of special speech recognition equipment, your computer can be taught to recognize up to 64 words or phrases and it will respond according to how you have programmed it to respond. Sounds strange, but it is true.

Heuristics, a small company in Los Altos, California, has developed an under-$300 speech recognition system that can be added to some of today's personal computers. One computer user has taught his computer to recognize enough phrases so that he can communicate with his deaf wife over the telephone. When he calls, she simply holds the phone next to a microphone that is connected to the computer as part of the speech recognition system. The computer prints out what it hears.

As this technology progresses, you'll be able to dictate to your computer. It will translate your dictation into written text.

The limitations of today's speech recognition equipment are the size of its vocabulary and the fact that the computer can only recognize one voice. To set up your vocabulary, you type the word or phrase into the computer and then speak it into the microphone. The computer is then programmed to print out this word or phrase or it can be programmed to execute any number of functions. In the future, when the waitress at the local cafe hollers out, "Two over easy with browns," a computer will automatically type up a bill for two eggs and hash brown potatoes. This information can be stored at the cash register so that no paper need change hands. Sounds incredible, but it is true.

Calculate Your Life Expectancy

In the November 1977 issue of *Kilobaud* magazine there is a program written by Terrence Lukas that can be used in most personal computers to calculate your life expectancy. Of course, no one can accurately predict how long you will live, but there are many unknown and known factors that seem to have a definite effect on this. Starting with individuals who are at least 20 years old, the computer first determines your life expectancy from your present age and sex. It then asks you a series of questions about your heredity, your health and diet, your education and occupation, and your life-style. Some sample questions are:

"DID ANY OF YOUR GRANDPARENTS, PARENTS, BROTHERS, OR SISTERS DIE OF A HEART ATTACK OR STROKE BEFORE AGE 50?"

"HOW MANY POUNDS OVERWEIGHT ARE YOU?"

"HOW MANY DRINKS DO YOU HAVE EACH DAY?"

"DO YOU EXERCISE MODERATELY—JOG, BIKE RIDE, TAKE LONG WALKS, SWIM—AT LEAST 2 OR 3 TIMES WEEK?"

"ARE YOU A MUSICIAN, ARCHITECT, OR PHARMACIST?"

The computer explains this last question by telling you that professionals—with the exception of musicians, architects, and pharmacists—usually live longer than most people. The reason for this is unknown, but statistical studies show it to be true.

Computer programs like this are designed to make people

think, take stock of their situations, and hopefully change their life-styles. For instance, if you are a heavy smoker, you can run the program twice to find out how much longer your life expectancy would be if you gave up smoking. And no one need know the results. It's between you and the machine.

Calculate Your Bio-rhythm

You can use the computer to figure your bio-rhythm or that of a friend. All you have to do is enter your birthdate and the computer will tell you how your emotional, physical, and intellectual abilities rate on any particular day. It will also draw a chart on the screen showing the pattern of these three factors for any particular month.

Although the reliability of bio-rhythms has been challenged, just for fun, let's assume that these charts are absolutely valid. The Super Bowl is coming up and you want to place a heavy bet on your favorite team. Suppose you have the birthdates of all the important players on both teams. Using the computer, you could examine the bio-rhythms of each player and analyze the probability of success on both sides. A quick way to investigate the possible validity of this procedure would be to enter Joe Namath's birthday into the computer and see what his bio-rhythm was on the day he led the New York Jets to their upset victory over the Baltimore Colts in Super Bowl III. I haven't done this, but it would be interesting to try it out. I wonder how Thomas Jefferson was feeling on July 4, 1776?

Stock Analysis

I haven't yet seen the personal computer used for comprehensive stock analysis but surely there are intelligent people busily at work on it. What I have seen are computers that will keep a record of your securities, including such relevant information as ownership (husband or wife, son or daughter, or any combination), name of the security, number of shares, cost, date of purchase, dividend, and recent quote. The computer can then analyze your dividends as to their value per share and so forth. It can also print out or display a chart showing you the current status of your portfolio, including the price at which you bought the stock, its current value, and your total loss or gain. Perhaps by the time you read this book, someone will have figured out how to use a personal computer to analyze the stock market, telling you what stocks are likely to rise, fall and remain stable. It could be worth a fortune.

Drawing Pictures

You can instruct the personal computer to draw pictures on a screen or to print them out on a line printer. Some personal computers are designed to be connected to color TV sets so you can vary the color as well as draw lines. The major drawback to this is that most television monitors have relatively poor resolution. Their pictures are made up of tiny squares called dot patterns and these squares are relatively large. A circle drawn on a TV screen looks more like a series of stairsteps than like a smooth line. Still, drawing with a computer can be great fun for you and your children.

Simulation

For years computer scientists have been using computers to simulate real or imagined events. Before a newly designed airplane ever leaves the ground, it has been "flown" thousands of times under all kinds of conditions by a computer. Of course, it isn't always possible to predict all the possibilities, and sometimes a small bit of vital information can be overlooked by the people who are programming the computer; yet this provides the designers with important data and probably saves millions of dollars and millions of man-hours, to say nothing of an occasional life or two.

For the owner of a personal computer, simulation programs can be used as learning exercises or for fun. One of the most popular computer games is a simulation called Lunar Landing. In this particular game you are challenged by the computer to figure the proper fuel allocation of a rocket ship that is landing on the moon. The trick is to use the fuel up at a rate where the craft can land safely at a nice slow speed. Use too much fuel at the wrong time and your craft will crash into the moon, killing everyone aboard.

With the advent of low-cost computers, one can easily imagine the literally thousands of exciting simulation programs that will be written for students and for people who simply want to have fun while learning. At least 100,000 people in the United States play noncomputerized war games on game boards that are not really very realistic. With a computer, these games can be programmed so that you have to keep track of logistical problems such as the amounts of ammunition, bandages, food, gasoline, shoes, and other supplies your troops have. Current game board war simulation games allow each side to see the troop positions of the enemy. With a computer, this could be hidden and each side would have to rely on scouting reports, enemy contact, and casualty figures to know what the other side was up to.

Rick Loomis, who is president of Flying Buffalo, a company in Scottsdale, Arizona, that keeps track of complex games with active players spread hundreds of miles apart, is presently working on a huge simulation game called "The World Game." The computer controlling this game will be in one location with players using mail, phone, or telegraph to report their moves from remote locations throughout the world. Small countries will be played by individual players, while larger countries will be played by groups of players. Some players will be presidents, dictators, generals, capitalists, criminals, and even subversives.

One can easily imagine that each player in "The World Game" could have his or her own personal computer on which to analyze and process moves. Instead of mailing each move or group of moves into the central computer, the players would mail in cassette tapes or better yet, relay them by telephone or radio beams. As Loomis envisions this game, people will become so involved that they may even "will" their positions to their heirs when they die.

As anyone who has visited an arcade game room at a shopping center lately will tell you, innovative companies are using microcomputers for all kinds of fascinating simulations. You can drive a race car, play baseball, shoot an antiaircraft gun, etc. The same technology that has brought about the personal computer has also brought about these new fun games.

The SFS Walletsize is a computer simulation of a lunar lander craft. (*Courtesy 2005AD, Inc.*)

While most of the arcade games are rather limited in scope (reflecting our short attention spans), one company in Philadelphia, called 2005AD, has built a space shuttle simulator called the SFS Walletsize that has been demonstrated at various personal computing events around the country. With three television screens, the player sees a three-dimensional picture as he attempts to land the craft on a lunar platform or dock it with another spacecraft. This simulated space shuttle has been designed to reflect the realities of flight physics and can be programmed to do any number of maneuvers.

Educate Your Children

Oftentimes I will pick up my daughter from school at 3 P.M. and then let her play in my office until it is time to go home. At first this was a bit of an inconvenience for me because I had to constantly find things for her to do so that I could concentrate my energies on business. But thanks to the computer, I have licked this problem and also given her something to do that is both fun and educational.

One of the programs I have written goes like this:

HELLO, MARA, DID YOU HAVE A GOOD DAY? ENTER 1 FOR YES AND 2 FOR NO.

Assuming that she answers 1 for yes, the computer then asks:

WOULD YOU LIKE TO PLAY WITH ME? ENTER 1 FOR YES AND 2 FOR NO.

If Mara answers 2 for the first question, the computer prints a consoling message and then asks her if she wants to play. If she answers 2 (no) to the second question, the program ends. She can then enter a different program into the computer (blackjack is one of her favorites) or find something else to do. Assuming she answers yes, the computer then says:

Aaron and Mara have fun learning with the aid of this personal computer.

WOULD YOU LIKE TO PLAY ADDITION (1), SUBTRAC-
TION (2), MULTIPLICATION (3), DIVISION (4), OR
WOULD YOU LIKE TO HELP ME WRITE A STORY (5)?
ENTER THE ANSWER FOR THE GAME YOU WOULD
LIKE TO PLAY.

If Mara wants to play subtraction, the computer randomly
selects subtraction problems for her to solve. When she gets
the right answer, it says "GOOD ANSWER, MARA, WOULD
YOU LIKE TO TRY ANOTHER ONE?" When she gets the
wrong answer, the computer says, "TRY AGAIN, MARA. YOU
CAN DO IT."

The other arithmetic games work the same way. The story
game is a program in which Mara selects nouns, verbs, and
other parts of speech to fill in the blanks of a computer-
generated story.

The advantage of the computer in this learning situation is that it gives the student an immediate response. It's fun, of course, and nobody needs to know when you enter an incorrect answer.

Learning About Computers

You can use a computer simply to learn about computers. As the computer industry grows, and it is growing faster than any other industry, the need for trained people who know about computers grows, too. Today, a career in computer programming or computer engineering or the many other related computer jobs can be very rewarding, and a qualified person can work almost anywhere. Just look at the want ads in your local newspaper. Be sure to check out those top-dollar salaries, too.

Many people build their own computers from kits using soldering irons and basic electronic assembly techniques. Following the step-by-step instructions that many manufacturers provide, you can save significant money over the price of preassembled computers and learn all about the internal makeup of the computer. It is not recommended that you try this unless you've had some previous experience building electronic kits. You can get this experience by building one of the many fine electronic kits available from Heathkit. Be careful that you deal with a reputable company if you get into this. Also, it is a good idea to buy the instruction manual before you buy the kit. Some companies, including Heathkit, will sell you the instruction manual and then deduct this price from the price of the kit if you decide to go ahead.

If working for another company is not your thing, there are plenty of opportunities to start your own computer company. Computer service companies abound and the need for them is growing daily. In fact, it is one of the easiest areas to get involved with without investing all of your life savings. Computer service companies are usually not capital-intensive. This means you don't have to buy a lot of equipment and supplies just to get started. For example, compare the price of a computer system to the price of stocking a retail clothing store.

Other Applications

Consider the following scenario:

7:20 A.M.   Your personal computer turns on your clock radio.

7:30 A.M.   The voice synthesizer interfaced to your personal computer tells you it's Monday and it's time to get up. It reminds you that last Monday you were 45 minutes late to the office and your boss won't like it if you're late again.

7:31 A.M.   You tell your computer that you don't care what your boss thinks, you're going to sleep for another 15 minutes.

7:46 A.M.   Your personal computer sounds an alarm. To turn the alarm off, you have to get up and walk into the study where the computer is (you've planned it this way).

7:48 A.M.   The computer turns on the shower, adjusting it to the specified temperature.

7:58 A.M.   Your computer activates the coffee pot and the electric frying pan. Breakfast will be ready in 5 minutes.

8:12 A.M.   Your computer activates the garage door opener and starts your car.

8:15 A.M.   You leave some last-minute instructions with the computer: If the doctor's office calls, you can instruct the computer to tell the doctor's computer that you can pay $25 now but the rest of the bill won't come in for a couple of weeks.

8:20 A.M.   You leave for work. The computer closes the garage door, turns off the lights, lowers the thermostat, and activates the burglar alarm system.

This may sound strange to you, but many personal computer users are interfacing their machines to their lighting systems, water systems, heating systems, etc. Accomplishing this requires a great deal of time and some knowledge on your part, but it is being done and will someday be packaged and marketed so that everyone can do it.

While it is true that personal computers can't do everything, there is really no end to the number of possible applications. The only restriction is the imagination and know-how of their owners. Once you have a personal computer, chances are you will think of something to do with it that has never been done before. After all, it is just a tool. It has some limited intelligence, but it lacks the imagination of the human brain. Imagination is the part you provide.

3

INSIDE COMPUTERS

Today there is little reason for the mystery that surrounds computers. Computers come in many shapes, colors, and sizes. To look at them, you'd think they were different from each other and very complex. Actually, all computers are basically the same and really rather simple.

Large computers that fill up rooms of space and cost millions of dollars are called *maxicomputers*. They are used primarily by large institutions such as government agencies, schools, scientific laboratories and big businesses.

Medium-sized computers, called *minicomputers*, are about the size and shape of a standard refrigerator. They cost as little as $15,000 and as much as $150,000, depending upon their capabilities and the slickness of the sales organizations selling them. Minicomputers are used by smaller institutions such as businesses with sales volumes between $5 million and $20 million. In many cases, a larger institution might have several minicomputers servicing its different subdivisions.

Small computers are called *microcomputers*, or more popularly, *personal computers*. They are typically desk-top units a little bigger than an office typewriter. They are used by individuals such as teachers, students, housewives, doctors, accountants, and by small institutions such as retail stores, real estate offices, and homes. Their cost is anywhere from $300 to $10,000. In this book, obviously, we are concerned mostly with microcomputers.

When computers as we know them today were relatively new (about 25 years ago), they could only be used by people who understood binary codes and machine language instructions. To use a computer, you had to understand in minute detail how the computer actually worked. Today, knowledge of the inside of a computer and how it works can be useful much in the same way that knowledge of the inside of a car and how it works can be useful. If you want to repair or modify either your car or your computer, you can save money by doing it yourself, oftentimes doing it faster and better. But, when it comes to *using* a computer, knowledge of what goes on inside the box is not necessary.

All computers are machines—simple arrangements of electronic parts or components. The source of their power is

All computers are simple arrangements of electronic parts, as you can see from this shot of the inside of an Xitan personal computer from Technical Design Labs. (*Courtesy Technical Design Labs*)

that they extend the capabilities of the human mind in much the same way as the steam engine extended what man could do with his muscles.

Information that goes into the computer is called *input;* information that comes back out of the machine is called *output.* Inside the computer, the information is either stored or the computer changes, adds to, or subtracts from it. One simple definition of a computer might be that it is a machine that takes information called input, processes it, and sends it back out in a form called output.

ON or OFF

To understand something about how computers actually process information, you need only realize that computers are based on the simple idea that an electric current can be either on or off. Computers work with information in the form of a code consisting of only two digits, a 1 and a 0. To the computer, the presence of an electric current represents a 1 and the absence of an electric current represents a 0.

The number system we are all familiar with is called a base 10 number system. It consists of 10 symbols (0 through 9). It was developed simply because man has ten fingers to count with.

The computer works with a number system that only has two symbols, a 0 and a 1. This number system is called a base 2 or binary number system.

Actually, to use a computer you don't need to know a thing about binary numbers. While computers are very useful in solving math-oriented problems, one myth we need to dispel right away is that you have to be a "math genius" to use a computer. You don't really have to know a thing about math to use a computer. *The importance of binary numbers is that they form the basis of how a computer actually works.*

Binary numbers in the form of electric current where the presence of a current is a 1 and the absence of a current is a 0 are fed into the computer. These binary numbers have been coded so that they represent any number, alphabetic character, punctuation mark, or special symbol. Usually this is accomplished by dividing the binary numbers into units of 8, which computer people refer to as *bytes*. Each byte of information then represents a code similar to the following:

A = 11 0001	J = 10 0001	S = 01 0010
B = 11 0010	K = 10 0010	T = 01 0011
C = 11 0011	L = 10 0011	U = 01 0100
D = 11 0100	M = 10 0100	V = 01 0101
E = 11 0101	N = 10 0101	W = 01 0110
F = 11 0110	0 = 10 0110	X = 01 0111
G = 11 0111	P = 10 0111	Y = 01 1000
H = 11 1000	Q = 10 1000	Z = 01 1001
I = 11 1001	R = 10 1001	

Using this code, the words "personal computing" would look like this:

P	E	R	S	O	N
10 0111	11 0101	10 1001	01 0010	10 0110	10 0101
A	L				
11 0001	10 0011				
C	O	M	P	U	T
11 0011	10 0110	10 0100	10 0111	01 0100	01 0011
I	N	G			
11 1001	10 0101	11 0111			

Each digit of the binary numbers fed into the computer, 0 or 1, is referred to as a *bit*. Personal computers generally use 8-bit codes. The two bits not used in the above codes are used by the computer to supply other information such as whether a number is positive or negative. Some people like to call personal computers "8-bit byte machines." Larger computers have 16-bit bytes, 32-bit bytes, 64-bit bytes, etc.

If you pursue your interest in computers, you'll run into the terms *bit* and *byte* quite frequently. The largest chain of computer retail stores in the United States is called *the* Byte Shops, while the first and largest computer hobbyist magazine is called *Byte*. One of the features in *Byte* is "BYTE's Bits."

Two Kinds of Information

There are only two basic kinds of input information that can be put into the computer. One kind is called a *program*. The other kind is called *data*. A program is really a set of step-by-step instructions to the computer telling it what to do with the data. The data can then be numbers, characters from the alphabet, or symbols. Once the program is finished processing the data, the results are stored in the computer's memory or sent out of the computer in the form of output. To understand how this really works we need to examine the inside of a typical computer.

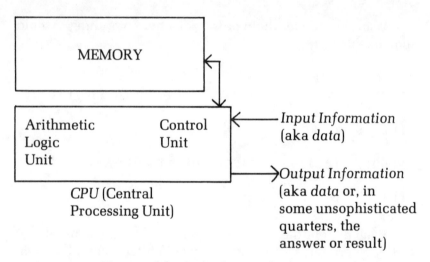

Diagram of the inside of a typical computer

The CPU

The computer has two basic units. One unit is the computer's *memory* and the other unit is called its *central processing unit* or CPU. The CPU is where the computer does its computing. It is divided into two areas, one called the *arithmetic/logical unit* and the other called the *control unit*. The CPU is the brain of a computer.

Control Unit

The *control unit* is like the switchboard Lily Tomlin uses in her comedy sketch about the telephone operator. It directs the binary data, sending some to the arithmetic/logical unit, some to the memory unit, and some out of the computer. The speed, accuracy, and timing of this modern-day switchboard, plus the enormous number of signals it can handle in a short period of time, is one important key to the power of computers. The control unit is a Lily Tomlin who never forgets, never dallies to polish her nails, and has several thousand hands, each of them much, much quicker than the hands of a clever magician or successful pickpocket.

Arithmetic/Logical Unit

The *arithmetic/logical unit* is where the binary data are acted upon; where they are changed according to program instructions, which are also passed along to it from the control unit. Surprisingly, this arithmetic/logical unit is not as smart as you might expect it to be. While it can add two binary numbers, it can't subtract, multiply, or divide them. A computer has about the mental capability of a burro with a few important exceptions.

Basically, a computer makes up for its limited mentality with speed. To multiply numbers, it simply adds them up at an incredible speed. To subtract or divide numbers, it uses a math technique called "complementary arithmetic." In binary arithmetic, you can subtract one number from another by taking its "one's complement" and adding that number to the number being subtracted from. What this means is simply changing the 0s to 1s and vice versa. Then, you add a 1 to the answer and ignore any carry digit on the left. For example:

SUBTRACTION		COMPLEMENTARY ARITHMETIC
1010 (10)		1010
- 1000 (8)	=	+ 0111 (complement of 1000)
10 (2)		0001 (ignoring carry on left)
		+ 1
		10 (2)

Machine Language Instructions

The arithmetic/logical unit can do a series of other dumb things like move a binary number from one location to another. Typically, it can do about 65 or more basic tasks with binary numbers. These tasks are called *machine language instructions* and are one of the measures of power among computers. Bigger, more powerful computers generally have more machine language instructions.

An example of a machine language instruction is *ADD L.* This instruction tells the arithmetic/logical unit to add the binary number at location *L* to the binary number in its *accumulator.* The accumulator is the actual part of the arithmetic/logical unit where binary numbers are added. *SUB L* means subtract (by means of complementary arithmetic) the binary number at location *L* from the binary number in the accumulator. The locations where binary numbers are stored in the arithmetic/logical unit are referred to as *registers.* One difference between CPU's is the number of registers in their arithmetic/logical units. It is the manipulation of binary numbers from these registers to the accumulator that serves as the basis for how computers think.

What Makes Computers Smart

If computers are so dumb, what makes them so smart? One thing, which I referred to already, is speed. The other is memory. Computers never forget (with one exception, which I'll explain later), and they have the capacity to remember and instantly recall an enormous amount of information. Aside from this, they are tireless. Imagine a human being trying to add by pencil and paper the total of all the bets placed in one day of racing at Aqueduct. Sooner or later, the human will tire or be distracted and make a mistake. *Computers do not make mistakes.* Contrary to popular opinion, there is no such thing as computer error. Computers always do exactly what we tell them to do. Thus, computer errors are really human errors. The computer will make a mistake when there is a mistake in the computer program that was written by a human.

To illustrate the speed of computers, imagine that you've just spilled a cup of coffee. By the time the coffee reaches the floor, a fairly large computer could do the following: 1) debit 2000 checks to 300 different bank accounts; 2) examine the electrocardiograms of 100 patients and alert a physician to possible trouble; 3) score 150,000 answers on 3000 examinations and evaluate the questions for effectiveness; and 4) figure the payroll for a company with 1000 employees.

Computer Memory

Computer memory can be either *internal memory* or *external memory*. Internal memory, often referred to as *core memory,* is the memory a computer has inside the box it comes in. The typical microcomputer has 4000 to 65,000 bytes of internal memory. This means it can store 4000 to 65,000 eight-bit binary codes. Computer people refer to a unit of 1000 as *1K.* Thus, when you look at computer literature or talk to your local computer retailer, you'll discover that one of the characteristics of the computers you're looking at is that they have *4K, 8K, 12K,* etc., bytes of memory. Actually, 1K of memory is 1024 bytes of memory (a bit of confusion thrown in to keep you in the dark about computers). There are good reasons for 1K of memory being 1024 bytes instead of 1000 bytes, but for all practical purposes, it is nothing to worry about. Over the years 1K has come to mean 1000. Computer people will sometimes use this designation when talking about things other than memory. They say such things as, "Did you see my new Porsche? I got it for only 15K." This brings up another thing about computer people. Because they have, up until now, been the only ones to really understand computers, they have been able to demand high salaries. It is not unusual for a computer programmer with four years of college and only a couple years of on-the-job experience to be drawing a salary of 30K to 40K per year. In many large institutions that are heavily dependent upon computers, the computer programmer will find himself rising quickly to the position of vice-president or becoming a member of the board of directors. That is because he has knowledge that no one else has and if the company loses him, the company could be in deep trouble. Chances are, he has programmed the company's computers in a manner that only he understands. Unfortunately for computer programmers, books like this one will change all that. Eventually, everyone will know how to use a computer.

The internal memory of a computer is called core memory because originally this memory consisted of magnetic cores made of tiny rings of magnetic material strung on grids of fine wire. Many of the maxicomputers still in use today use this method of internal memory. Information is stored on these cores by sending pulses of electric current through the wires that magnetize each core in one of two directions (thus, each core can represent either a "0" or a "1"). These cores retain their magnetic state until another pulse is sent through them reversing the state.

Today, because of the dramatic developments in semiconductor technology, internal memory is stored on chips of silicon as small as an eighth of an inch square. Each of these chips of silicon represents as many as 1000 electric circuits. Later we will examine these chips, often referred to as *integrated circuits* or *IC chips,* in more detail. They are the basic technological reason for the dramatic reduction in the size and cost of both computers and calculators.

One problem with using ICs for internal memory is that they are volatile. This means that once the electric current going into the computer is turned off, the memory stored in these chips is forgotten. One way around this problem is never to turn the computer off; the other way is to store vital information in *external* memory. Advances in a new technology called *bubble memory* will eliminate this problem for good, but the implementation of this technology is still a few years off.

Internal memory then is that memory which is used by the computer to solve immediate problems. The program and the data that the computer is working on are stored in internal memory where the CPU has instant access to it. The amount of internal memory you have is important if you are using a computer to run fairly long, complicated programs. While most programs you will be concerned with initially will run comfortably in 4K or 8K of memory, there are programs that are much longer than this. When you buy a computer, you'll want to know if its memory is expandable. Altair-type computers, which we referred to earlier, have memory expandability up to 65K, while the Radio Shack computer, which we will examine in more detail in a later chapter, can only be expanded up to 16K.

External memory is memory that is stored outside the computer. Many home computer users use magnetic tape to store external memory. Most microcomputers are made so that you can connect a standard audio cassette tape recorder to them. Memory storage on audio tape is accomplished by changing the electronic or digital signals in the computer to audio tones. Thus, instead of a 1 representing an electronic pulse and a 0 representing the absence of an electronic pulse, on an audio tape a high tone represents a 1 and a low tone represents a 0.

The IBM 5100 Portable Computer uses a specially designed magnetic tape cartridge for external memory storage. Most home computers use the less expensive, standard cassette tape and cassette tape recorder. (*Courtesy IBM*)

To understand the need for external memory, let's say that you want to keep track of all your household possessions on a computer so that in case of fire or theft you will be able to provide your insurance agent with accurate information. Unless this was the sole use you had for your computer, you would not be able to keep this information on the computer's internal memory. You certainly wouldn't want to risk the possibility of losing the information if the electricity went out in your neighborhood or if someone accidentally turned off your computer. In this case, you could store both the list of your possessions and the computer program that instructs the computer how to use the list on audio tape. When you buy something new for your house, you simply "load" the program from the audio tape into your computer's internal memory so that it can be updated. Doing this is a very simple procedure that we will outline later. Once you have updated the information, you can once again store it on tape for later use.

One of the disadvantages of using an audio cassette recorder for external storage is that the information on the tape itself is stored *sequentially*. This means that in order for the computer to find a particular bit of information, it must examine all of the information on the tape up to that point. This process is slow and unworkable in some applications.

An even better method of storing external information is with a device called a *floppy disk system*. This is simply another box about the size and shape of the computer which you can hook up or *interface* to your computer. The word "interface" is another one of those terms computer people like to bandy about. It simply means connecting an external device (anything from a cassette recorder to a floppy disk to a typewriter) to a computer.

In a floppy disk system, computer information is stored on a plastic disk that looks very much like a standard record except that it is square shaped. When a particular piece of information is needed by the computer, it can be located and retrieved directly instead of sequentially. The disk spins inside the box, called a drive, at a speed of over 300 rpm; a magnetic recording head inside the drive also moves back and forth.

On a floppy disk, external memory is stored on plastic disks called diskettes. This device can be interfaced to many personal computers and is far superior to magnetic tape storage. (*Courtesy Midwest Scientific Instruments*)

Usually any information on a floppy disk can be located within a half second.

There are other forms of external memory including punched paper tape similar to that found on a Teletype™ machine; punched computer cards, which we have all run across one time or another; hard disks, which store more information than floppies and are made of metal instead of plastic; and reel-to-reel tapes. However, the computers we are concerned with by and large use audio tape or floppy disks for mass storage.

A Computer System

In the beginning of this chapter we said that a computer is a machine that takes information called input, processes it, and sends it back out in a form called output. No computer is complete without a device for feeding input into the computer and a device for retrieving output from the computer. Now that we have examined in some detail what actually goes on

As with stereo systems, you can go the "component route" with personal computers. The Altair business system pictured here includes an Altair computer and two floppy disk systems in the cabinet on the left, and a video terminal and a line printer all fitted nicely into custom office furniture. (*Courtesy Pertec Computer Corporation*)

inside a computer, we need to focus our attention on these input/output devices. Together with an external storage device, they make up what is called a *computer system.*

Input devices (typewriter style keyboards, card readers, teletypewriters), output devices (line printers, CRT's, television screens), and external storage devices are collectively referred to as computer *peripherals.* Peripherals are devices that are hooked or interfaced to a computer.

An easy way to understand the concept of a computer system is to think of a stereo system. If the amplifier in a stereo system is considered to be the main part of the system, then the turntable and the speakers are peripherals. The turntable is an input device and the speakers are output devices. Like stereo systems, computers come in many different configurations. Some computers already have built-in keyboards just as some stereo systems have built-in turntables. Some computers also have built-in TV screens that serve as output devices, just as some stereo systems have built-in speakers.

All these peripheral devices *plus the computer* are sometimes called *computer hardware.* The programs that tell the computer what to do are called *computer software.* To make matters worse, there is also *computer firmware* (see chapter 5), which is halfway between hardware and software.

4

MICROPROCESSORS AND OTHER COMPONENTS

In the previous chapter, we said that computers are simple arrangements of parts or components. We also said that the CPU is the brain of the computer. Until a few years ago, the CPU consisted of many components. In maxicomputers and many minicomputers this is still the case. However, in the microcomputers we are concerned with, the CPU is one single component called a *microprocessor*.

A typical microprocessor is about 5/8 inch wide by 2 inches long by 1/8 inch thick. It has about 40 small pins called electrical connections coming out of its sides making it look somewhat like a futuristic electronic spider.

Microprocessors are manufactured out of a semimetal called silicon. This substance, which has some properties of carbon, is present in the earth in greater amounts than any element with the exception of oxygen. As silicon dioxide, it is found in sand, flint, quartz, and opal. As complex silicates of aluminum, iron, magnesium, and other metals, it is in nearly all clays, rocks, and soils.

Through a complex photographic reduction and chemical process, silicon is manufactured into small chips approximately 1/4 inch square by 1/16 inch thick. The plastic case that microprocessors are packaged in accounts for the dif-

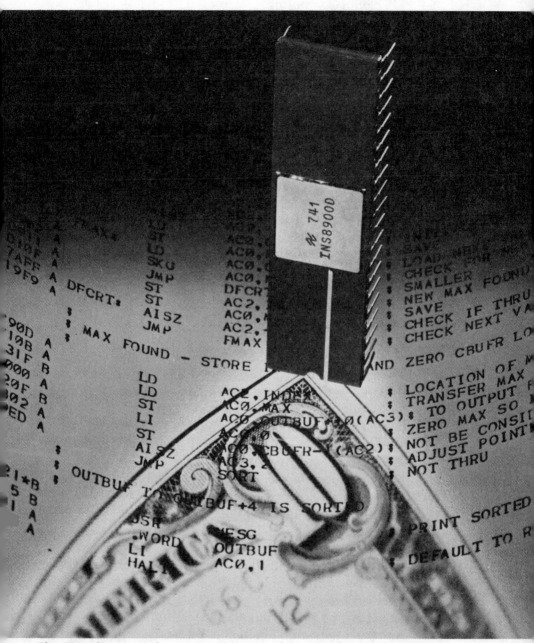

The CPU of a personal computer is contained on a single microprocessor. Since these devices began selling for as little as $10 in large quantities, the price of computers has dropped drastically. (*Courtesy National Semiconductor Corporation*)

ference between these dimensions and the ones above. What is important about the chips is that they contain the equivalent of approximately 10,000 electronic circuits and resistors! You've probably heard stories of people engraving the Lord's Prayer on the head of a pin. Well, compared to what is being done with miniaturized circuits, you ain't seen nothing yet, as the saying goes.

Microprocessors

The first microprocessor, or "computer on a chip," was manufactured by the Intel Corporation in 1968. Since that time, at least 100 different microprocessors have been manufactured. When the Intel 8080, which serves as the CPU for the Altair computer, was introduced in 1974, it sold for approximately $350 (price varied according to quantity). Today, an Intel 8080 microprocessor chip costs less than $10.

Some of the microprocessors, like the Intel 8080, the Motorola 6800, the Mostek 6502, and the Zilog Z-80, are used in personal computers, while many others are used in more specific applications such as video games and programmable handheld calculators. In the not-too-distant future, virtually every appliance you operate will have a microprocessor in it. Already they are being used in a wide range of products from automobiles to microwave ovens.

A microprocessor can be used to turn an ordinary appliance into an "intelligent" appliance. One turntable recently introduced has the capacity to play individual selections on a record instead of playing the whole side. If you want to hear songs 3 and 5, you simply press the corresponding buttons and the microprocessor-controlled tonal arm finds the proper grooves. If you want to play selection 5 twice, then 3 once, and 5 four more times, you can program the turntable to remember this sequence and it will follow your instructions.

Another interesting intelligent appliance is the Computerphone 370 from Utility Verification Corporation in Commack, New York. This phone looks very much like a standard office touch-tone telephone except that it has a digital readout that

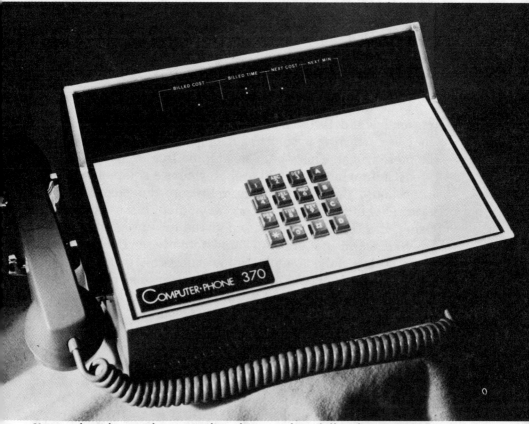

You can keep better tabs on your long distance phone bill with a Computer-phone 370 from Utility Verification Corporation. *(Courtesy Utility Verification Corporation)*

fits on a panel just above the dialing buttons. When you are not using the phone, the readout acts as a digital clock and calendar. When you are using the phone, the readout displays the cost of any long-distance call you are making. Fifteen seconds before the next billing time is to occur, the display begins flashing. In addition to calculating any long-distance calls, the phone keeps track of the cost of all calls made during a month including the toll calls and unit calls you make in some areas. When you purchase a computer-phone, you enter the home/office base number, local time, and date. The clock and the built-in ten-year calendar take over from there, automatically changing rates for holidays, weekends, etc. The

memory chip inside the phone contains all the rate information for the entire country. When Ma Bell periodically changes
her rate structure, Utility Verification Corporation will simply
send you a new memory chip that reflects these changes.

The theory of the Computer-phone, which seems to be
perfectly valid, is that if people are instantly aware of the costs
they are incurring when using the telephone, they can learn to
be more frugal. This would seem to be true in many different
areas. Before long, you will probably have a computer panel in
your house that keeps an up-to-the-moment record of your
electricity bill, your gas bill, and any other utilities you may be
using. If a flashing red light appeared every time you turned
up your thermostat and you could actually see the increase in
your costs as the digital readout mercilessly ticked away,
chances are you would become more energy conscious.

As if keeping track of "How does Bell toll thee?" (as a recent advertisement for the Utility Verification Corporation put

The TeleCoster I retails for under $100 and can save you money on long dis-
tance phone bills. (*Courtesy Utility Verification Corporation*)

it) weren't enough, the Computer-phone will automatically dial the last entered telephone number. If you call someone and the line is busy, the Computer-phone will keep dialing until you get through. Priced at $399, this product is primarily intended for businesses. However, UVC also markets a product called the TeleCoster I that looks very much like a handheld calculator. Retailing for $99.95, this device will aid you in calculating long-distance calls and essentially serve the same purpose as a Computer-phone. One drawback to the TeleCoster is that you have to enter cost data for every area code and exchange before placing a call. The company does provide you with a handy directory for your area, but this difficulty will limit the market potential of the TeleCoster.

It is no wonder that people today are so convenience oriented. The extent of this phenomenon is illustrated by the advent of a new microprocessor-controlled color television set (manufactured by Sharp Electronics) that allows viewers to

The microprocessor controlled, programmable television set from Sharp Electronics. (*Courtesy Sharp Electronics Corporation*)

Video games are beginning to look more like home computers. The model pictured here is playing a logical, number-guessing game with Channel F Video Entertainment System. (*Courtesy Fairchild Camera and Instrument Corporation*)

preset up to eight programs a day. The television has a built-in digital clock, an electronic tuner, and remote control. It will turn the evening news on at exactly five o'clock or "Happy Days" at eight or "CHiPs" at seven-thirty, depending on how you program it.

Video games are, of course, the most noticed of all the microprocessor-controlled appliances. Many of these products claim to be computers but really aren't. They have memory and can be programmed by the manufacturer, but they can't be programmed by the users and usually don't have keyboards for entering alphabetic characters.

One of the most popular of these is the Channel F Video Entertainment System manufactured by Fairchild. Its programs are on plug-in memory boards, which are cleverly disguised to look like tape cartridges. At the time of this writing, Fairchild offered 18 different kinds of these "Videocarts" at $19.95 each.

Some video games are beginning to look more like com-

The Bally Professional Arcade (*Courtesy Bally Manufacturing Corporation*)

puters as the technology advances, while some personal computers are also beginning to look more like video games. The most glaring example of the merger of these two products is the Bally Professional Arcade, which claims to be a "video game/computer system" capable of "remembering more and doing more than any other system now available."

Actually, the Bally appears to have started out as a video game and gradually has become more like a computer with the introduction of optional programming capability. However, its keyboard is a calculator style keyboard. Entering alphabetic characters requires two strokes of the keys. Perhaps, Bally will offer peripherals such as simple line printers and real keyboards and the game will become a real computer. But at the time of this writing, I can't say this is certain.

Not all microprocessor games are video games, of course, and one of the more interesting of these is the Checker Challenger manufactured by Fidelity Electronics, which, like Bally, is headquartered in Chicago. It is packaged in an attractive walnut case and has many interesting features including a "verification" key that displays the board position of each piece in case the pieces are knocked off the board or you get confused as to whether you've made a proper move.

The Checker Challenger (*Courtesy Fidelity Electronics*)

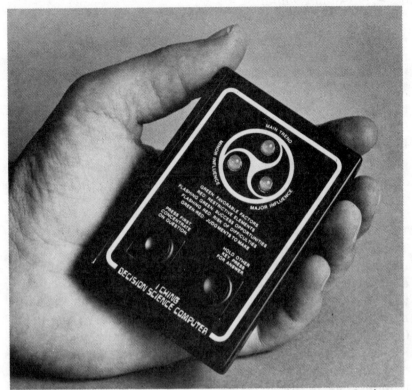

The I Ching Decision Science Computer (*Courtesy Solfan System, Inc.*)

The I CHING Decision Science "Computer" would seem to be for people who are heavily into horoscopes and other future-predicting sciences. Put your finger on the button, ask a question, and the I CHING will tell you the answer. Should I bet $500 on this next shot at the crap table? It is manufactured by Solfan System, Inc., of Mountain View, California.

The microprocessors in these products and in personal computers vary in speed and complexity. Some of them have more machine language instructions, different power supply requirements, etc. However, when you buy a personal computer, you really don't need to be too concerned about which microprocessor it has. What is more important about personal computers is how well they are supported by both hardware and software, what applications they can be used for, and how much they cost. The microprocessors mentioned earlier in this chapter have been around long enough to be fairly well supported in most computer systems. Engineers and programmers have been working with them long enough to have developed a wide range of applications. You do, however, need to be cautious if you buy a computer with a "new" and usually "revolutionary" microprocessor chip. It may be that the chip has a lot of speed and capability but hasn't been around long enough to have the support you'll want.

Other Kinds of Chips

Microprocessors aren't the only kinds of chips around. Two others are memory and interface chips. Most of the internal memory in a personal computer consists of RAM or random access memory chips. These chips, which can contain up to 16K bytes of memory, are called random access chips because you can both store and retrieve memory from them. Other memory chips, called ROM (read only memory) or PROM (programmable read only memory), generally come preprogrammed from the factory. The memory in them is permanent and, unlike RAM memory, nonvolatile. If your computer has some ROM memory in it, it will not forget when the power is turned off. These preprogrammed chips are used to store programming languages and special software.

(As with the case of *Byte*, there is also a computer hobbyist magazine called *ROM*. In fact, there is even a publication called the *Silicon Gulch Gazette*. The word "gulch" in this title refers to the fact that most electronics companies in the chip manufacturing business are located on the peninsula below San Francisco. This area, including Mountain View, Sunnyvale, and San Jose, California, is collectively referred to in the computer trade as "silicon gulch" or "silicon valley.")

In addition to microprocessor chips, memory chips and interface chips, the internal components of a computer are very much like the internal components of any electronic product. They include transistors, resistors, capacitors, and diodes which are collectively referred to as support circuitry for the chips.

Other Components

One group of components in all personal computers makes up the power supply for the system. This group of components includes a transformer that generally looks like the transformer found in a model electric railroad.

Some computers also have cooling fans because memory chips and many other components can develop problems if they become overheated. Tandy Corporation (Radio Shack) may have made a design mistake with its TRS-80 microcomputer by not including a fan. A TRS-80 with 4K of memory works fine, and not having a fan makes a computer quieter, but a TRS-80 with 16K of memory reportedly develops heat problems when left on for any length of time. Suddenly, funny letters appear on the TV screen and parts of the program you are working on simply disappear. Chances are that by the time you read this, Tandy will have corrected this problem.

5

SOFTWARE AND PROGRAMMING

Software is the instructions that tell computer hardware what to do. It is stored in many forms, including paper punch tape, magnetic tape, and floppy disks. When it is stored on permanent memory chips (including ROM, PROM, and many variations), it is called firmware.

The idea that led to the development of software was conceived in the 1880s by a young engineer in the United States Census Bureau, Herman Hollerith. His motivation for doing this was a crisis inside the bureau that came about when it took four years to tabulate the 1880 census. Unless something was done about this, the 1890 census would take much longer because the country was growing at a frantic pace. Census officials were genuinely afraid that the day was approaching when a 10-year census couldn't even be completed in 10 years.

Hollerith got his idea, which consisted of storing census data on punched cards, while standing in a railroad station watching the conductor punch tickets. He proposed that the bureau build an electromechanical counting machine that could tabulate the data on a punch card. Holes in the cards would be in patterns coded to represent numbers and letters.

The essential part of the original machine that Hollerith designed was a reading station built out of wire brushes. When

64

there was a hole in a card, one of the wire brushes would make contact causing an electric current to activate a counter.

Hollerith's machine worked so well that the bureau was able to tabulate the 1890 census in less than half the time it took to tabulate the 1880 census, even though the population had grown by 25 percent. Like so many government employees before and since, Hollerith got the bright idea that he could make money with this invention, so he left the government to found the Tabulating Machine Company. This company prospered for many years before it merged with two other companies to form Big Brother, IBM.

The early tabulating or business machines made by Hollerith and others weren't really much more sophisticated than a music box. They were built to perform a specific, limited, and *fixed* sequence of operations for each punch card. At first, they could read a card and add it to the counter. Later, "plug boards" were invented for multiplication, division, subtraction, and other functions. These plug boards could be interchanged, and soon there were libraries of plug boards available.

Tabulating machines with their plug boards were "variable hardware" machines: You could change the functions they performed by changing their plug boards. While these boards were close to the concept of modern-day software, it wasn't until 1945 that the single most important idea that actually made possible computers as we know them was introduced by the famous mathematician, Dr. John von Neumann. This idea was the concept of stored programs that could be entered into the computer with the same punch cards used to enter data (and later, by other means).

The Original Altair

When the Altair computer was introduced in January 1975, it was just a chunk of hardware. To program it, you had to enter binary codes into the machine using the front panel toggle switches. This type of programming, called *machine language programming*, required that you become familiar

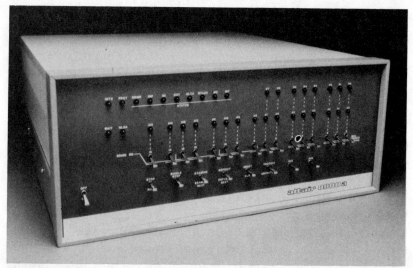

The original Altair, pictured here, had to be programmed by using the front panel switches. (*Courtesy Mits, Inc.*)

with the 65 basic operations and numerous variations of the microprocessor chip inside the computer. Simply adding two numbers together required 15 or so programming instructions. These machine language instructions were complicated and not much fun to work with. Had the personal computer stayed on this level, its popularity today would be almost zero, and only the most dedicated of electronics hobbyists would be working with them.

High-Level Languages

Fortunately, today you can program a personal computer without knowing a thing about machine language programming or binary numbers. This is made possible by high-level computer languages that allow you to communicate with the computer in ordinary English commands.

A high-level computer language is in itself a long set of instructions stored in the computer's memory. This set of instructions is either loaded into the computer each time you turn it on, or it is permanently stored inside on ROM or PROM memory chips (and thus is called firmware). In personal computers, these instructions usually take the form of an *inter-*

preter that directly translates English-type instructions into machine language instructions. Thus, when you tell a computer to print your name by entering the command PRINT "JACK," the interpreter translates your instructions into the necessary machine language program that will compel the computer to print your name.

There are about as many computer languages as there are human languages. This situation was brought about because the computer can do so many different applications that different languages were developed that better serve specific purposes. For instance, the computer language COBOL was written to serve the business community, while the language FORTRAN was written for the scientific community. Because the computer is currently used more for business purposes than any other purpose, COBOL is, by far, the most common language. Other popular languages include BASIC, APL, PL/M, FOCAL, and MUMPS.

With the advent of microcomputers, COBOL is likely to lose its first-place ranking because these new machines are by and large programmed in BASIC. BASIC, which stands for Beginner's All Purpose Symbolic Instruction Code, was developed by a group of students and professors in the early 1960s at Dartmouth College. The purpose of this development was to create a general purpose computer language that was easy for people to learn. Today, BASIC is the standard language among amateurs and hobbyists and in secondary schools. A large library of BASIC language programs is available.

The two drawbacks to BASIC are that, just as with most human languages, there are many different dialects of BASIC and some complicated programming techniques are very difficult (if not impossible) to implement in BASIC. However, for the time being it is the best language we've got for making computers popular. It is easy to learn, and people are constantly modifying and improving it.

BASIC will probably remain *the* computer language of the masses for some time simply because it is there. Like English, it isn't perfect, just well known and used. Many hobbyists and computer programmers would like to replace BASIC with a more perfect and even easier to use language, but as time goes by it will be harder and harder to change the course of events.

Still, work continues on new languages, and if any one language ever does win out over BASIC, it may very well be one called SMALLTALK. Developed at Xerox Palo Alto Research, SMALLTALK has far greater graphic capability than BASIC, and indeed, many of its commands are symbols, such as smiling faces and pointing hands instead of words. SMALLTALK is designed to be used on computer screens with very good resolution (up to a half million dots) and thus could be used for many sophisticated graphic applications including animation. Also, it is reportedly easier to find mistakes (a process called *debugging*) in a SMALLTALK program than in a BASIC program because the program is written in sections of individual entities called *processes*.

One drawback to SMALLTALK is the simple fact that Xerox hasn't seen fit to make it available to the public. Still, word about this new language is getting out and many hobbyists are pressuring Xerox to release it.*

Different BASICs

When BASIC language interpreters were first written for personal computers, the primary consideration was efficiency. For an Altair computer 4K of memory cost over $200, and not many hobbyists could afford to expand beyond 8K. A BASIC language had to be written that could operate within 4K of memory so that the average user would have enough memory left over to do some programming.

Dramatic reductions in the cost of computer memory (16K is now less than $200) and the use of personal computers in small businesses necessitated a change in emphasis from efficiency to capability. BASICs of 12K and 16K were developed to run on computers with floppy disk systems. These BASICs

*More information on SMALLTALK and on LAMBDA languages (of which SMALLTALK is one example) can be found in the book *The Home Computer Revolution*, by Ted Nelson, published by the author and distributed by The Distributors, 702 South Michigan, South Bend, Indiana 46618.

have powerful file commands that allow you to catalogue and reference large amounts of information including inventory records, accounts receivable, bowling league scores, or whatever you need of interest.

The smallest BASIC of all is *tiny* BASIC, which was developed by People's Computer Company in Menlo Park, California. This BASIC, which runs on less than 2K of memory, is powerful enough to be used for many educational programs and games.

Microsoft, the company that developed Altair BASIC, was founded by two college students: Bill Gates and Paul Allen. Shortly after seeing the cover article in the January 1975 issue of *Popular Electronics*, these students called Ed Roberts and asked him if he'd like to have a BASIC interpreter. He responded favorably and they went to work on the project using free computer time on one of the university's computers. About a month later they had a crude version of BASIC running on an Altair and since then Microsoft has developed into the leading software company in the personal computing business. Microsoft BASIC, noted for its efficiency and many powerful features, is used on many computers including Altair, PET, Ohio Scientific, NCR, and IMSAI, to name a few. A 12K BASIC for the TRS-80 computer from Radio Shack was being developed by Microsoft at the time of this writing.

The domination of the software market by Microsoft has the positive benefit of making many computers more compatible since they have similar BASICs. Of course, there are many other companies that have developed their own versions of BASIC, including Processor Technology, Apple, and North Star. The problem with having different BASICs is that a program written for one machine can't run on a different machine (with a different BASIC) without modifications. Computer companies in the personal computing field need to get together to standardize BASIC and to standardize floppy disk software and cassette interface software. This would open up the market for software companies to develop application programs which they could sell on cassette tapes and floppy disks.

When you buy a computer system you need to make sure

that its programming language is powerful enough to handle the applications you have in mind. Most all BASICs on the market are adequate for simple games and home applications, but many fall short when it comes to storing and retrieving large amounts of information. A computer store retailer or a member of a local computer club (see appendixes) would be a good person to talk to about this problem.

Other Software You Need to Know About

When software is permanently stored on read only memory (ROM) chips, it is called firmware. Most personal computers have what is called a *firmware monitor*. This software handles the input and output of data between the computer and peripheral devices such as cassette tape recorders, line printers, and CRTs. You cannot interface a computer to a line printer and expect the line printer to function without this software.

An *operating system* is an enlarged version of a monitor. Often this software is too large to be stored permanently on ROM chips, so it is stored on cassette tapes or floppy disks. A computer with a floppy disk needs to have a *disk operating system* that takes care of data transfer between the disk and the computer and allows information on the disk to be formatted. Usually, when you buy a disk drive, a disk operating system (DOS) comes as part of the package. Oftentimes, *disk BASIC* is also supplied. This is a BASIC with special commands for storing information on a disk and manipulating that information once it is stored.

Finally, there is *application software,* which is computer programs that have been written to solve particular problems. If you want to do small business bookkeeping on a computer, chances are you can buy a general ledger software application package that will handle this task. Usually these packages have been written to work for many different businesses and they can be modified to suit your own particular needs.

Computer Programming: Just How Hard Is It?

A computer program is a set of instructions to a computer telling it how to solve a particular problem. If you understand the limited set of instructions of a particular computer language like BASIC and how the language and the computer work together, then you can program a computer. What makes programming difficult is the fact that the computer can't solve any problem unless you tell it how. Thus if you can't figure out how the computer might go about solving something, you are in trouble.

In BASIC there are two kinds of instructions called *statements* and *commands*. To illustrate the difference, let's go back to the computer we used in the beginning of this book. As you may recall, this particular computer consisted of a cassette tape recorder, a keyboard, and a TV monitor. To turn it on, we simply push the red button on the TV monitor and the red button on the keyboard. The computer, which is cleverly hidden inside the keyboard case, responds with:

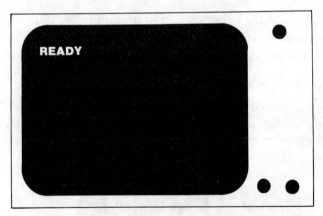

Since the particular computer in this example happens to be a Radio Shack TRS-80, the word *READY* tells us that the computer can immediately be programmed in BASIC because the BASIC language is contained inside the keyboard case in a ROM memory chip. (Some personal computers don't have this feature. To use these you must first load BASIC language

The computer used to write this programming lesson was the Radio Shack TRS-80. (*Courtesy Radio Shack*)

into the computer's memory via cassette tape, paper tape, or floppy disk. This procedure, which is fairly simple, is explained in the operator's instructions that come with these units.)

The word *PRINT* in BASIC can be either a statement or a command. If we enter the instruction PRINT "COMPUTER PROGRAMMING AIN'T SO HARD" into the computer, it will immediately respond with COMPUTER PROGRAMMING AIN'T SO HARD. Our TV screen will look like this:

READY
PRINT "COMPUTER PROGRAMMING
    AIN'T SO HARD."

COMPUTER PROGRAMMING
    AIN'T SO HARD.

READY

However, if we instead enter: 10 PRINT "COMPUTER PROGRAMMING AIN'T SO HARD," the computer will just sit still, patiently awaiting further instruction. By placing the number 10 in front of the word *PRINT*, we changed this instruction from a command to a statement. Commands are executed immediately, while statements aren't executed until the command RUN has been entered into the computer. Thus, if we follow our PRINT *statement* with the word *RUN*, the computer will respond with:

```
10 PRINT "COMPUTER
   PROGRAMMING AIN'T SO HARD."

RUN
COMPUTER PROGRAMMING
   AIN'T SO HARD.

READY
```

There are four parts to writing a computer program in BASIC. These parts include (1) *defining the problem;* (2) *data;* (3) *computing the data;* and (4) *outputting the answers.*

Just for kicks, let's consider the problem of figuring add-on, or as it is better known, simple interest rates. You just purchased a used car for $1800. You made a down payment of $500 and borrowed the rest of the money at an add-on rate of 16 percent over a period of 30 months. You want to know the answers to three questions:

1. What is the amount of interest you are going to pay?
2. What is the total amount of money owed?
3. What are the monthly payments going to be?

Guess what? We just did the first part; we defined the problem. We determined exactly what we want to know about this loan.

A computer doesn't really think in the sense that a human brain thinks. What a computer does is *manipulate data.*

Naturally, before a computer can do anything, it has to have data to manipulate. The data we want to input into the computer are the principal of the loan ($1800), the rate of interest (16 percent), and the time (30 months).

Once the data are entered into the computer, we have to tell it what to do with the data, or how to compute the data. From grade school arithmetic we know that the formula for figuring add-on interest is: *interest* equals *principal* times *rate* times *time* or $I = P \times R \times T$. Since *time* in this equation refers to the *number of years*, we have to divide our answer by 12, making the equation read: $I = P \times R \times T/12$. (To find the interest in our loan, we are going to instruct the computer to multiply *principal* times *rate* times *time* divided by 12.)

We also want to know what the *total payment* will be. Since the total payment is equal to the amount of the loan (the principal) plus the interest, our equation is *total payment* equals *principal* plus *interest* or $X = P + I$ (X being the unknown—total payment).

The final question we want the computer to answer is: What is the amount of our monthly payments? Since monthly payments are equal to the total payment divided by the number of months we have to pay off the loan, the equation is $M = X/T$ where M is equal to monthly payments.

Computers are really simpleminded beasts. They do exactly what we tell them to do, no more and no less. Unless we tell the computer to print out or display the answers of our problem, the computer will keep the answers to itself.

This takes us to the final part of writing a computer program, which is outputting the data. Let us review again the information we are seeking:

1. Total interest
2. Total amount owed
3. Monthly payments

The following program, once entered into the computer, will answer our questions. While at this point the program may look confusing to you, once we examine its various components, it should become clear.

```
NEW
10 LET P = 1300
20 LET T = 30
30 LET R = .16
40 LET I = P*T*R/12
50 LET X = P + I
60 LET M = X/T
70 PRINT "TOTAL INTEREST IS";I
80 PRINT "TOTAL MONEY OWED IS";X
90 PRINT "MONTHLY PAYMENTS ARE";M
```

(Notice in line 40 that the symbol for multiplication is an asterisk [*] instead of the traditional X. The reason for this is that the computer is not smart enough to figure out the difference between the letter X and the multiplication symbol X. The arithmetic symbols that the computer recognizes are " + " for addition, " − " for subtraction, "/" for division, and "*" for multiplication.)

BASIC Elements

As we mentioned in the beginning of this chapter, BASIC language offers only two formats for instructing the computer; these are statements and commands. A command is executed immediately while a statement is not executed until the computer has received the command *RUN*.

The number preceding a statement is called a *line number* and it tells the computer two things: (1) don't execute the instruction until the command *RUN* has been given; and (2) execute the instruction according to the order of the numbers. Had the first three statements in our program been entered into the computer:

```
20 LET T = 30
10 LET P = 1300
30 LET R = .16
```

they would still be executed beginning with line 10.

Typically line numbers can be any integer (no decimals) between 1 and 9999. When writing programs, it is a common practice to leave unused numbers between statements so that new statements can be inserted later.

The first line of our program is the command *NEW*. This instructs the computer to immediately clear its memory of any other data or programs. Without this instruction, the computer might confuse a program already in its memory with the one you are about to enter. If you want to save a particular program for later use, you must first transfer it to cassette tape, paper tape, or a floppy disk before you enter the *NEW* command.

The next six lines of the program are *LET* statements. These statements instruct the computer to assign a number or an equation to a letter whose proper mathematical term is a *variable*. In line 10, the number 1300 is assigned to the variable, *P*.

The first three *LET* statements in our program represent the part of the program called *inputting the data:*

```
10 LET P=1300
20 LET T=30
30 LET R=.16
```

The next three *LET* statements represent the part of the program called *computing the data:*

```
40 LET I=P*T*R/12
50 LET X=P+I
60 LET M=X/T
```

Once a number has been assigned to a variable, the variable can be used to represent the number throughout the remaining program. Thus, in statements 40 and 50, the variable *P* is still 1300.

The last three statements in the program are *PRINT* statements, which represent the last part of the program, *outputting the data:*

70 PRINT "TOTAL INTEREST IS"; *I*
80 PRINT "TOTAL MONEY OWED IS";*X*
90 PRINT "MONTHLY PAYMENTS ARE";*M*

A *PRINT* statement can be used to instruct the computer to display a number or the result of a computation, or it can instruct the computer to display a "string literal." These *PRINT* statements instruct the computer to display a *string literal* followed by a number.

A string literal, if you haven't already guessed, is a string of characters enclosed within quotation marks in a *PRINT* statement. It instructs the computer to print out the string of characters exactly as they are in the *PRINT* statement. In other words, to print them or display them literally.

Now that we've entered the program into the computer and examined its various elements, let's enter the *RUN* command and see what happens:

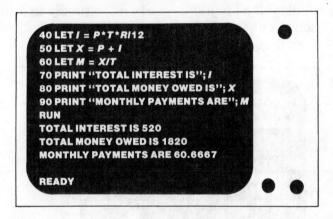

```
40 LET I = P*T*R/12
50 LET X = P + I
60 LET M = X/T
70 PRINT "TOTAL INTEREST IS"; I
80 PRINT "TOTAL MONEY OWED IS"; X
90 PRINT "MONTHLY PAYMENTS ARE"; M
RUN
TOTAL INTEREST IS 520
TOTAL MONEY OWED IS 1820
MONTHLY PAYMENTS ARE 60.6667

READY
```

Part of the program has moved off the screen and the computer has "output" the answer to our loan problem. Of course, the best way to learn how to program a computer is to actually sit down at a computer and do it. This program, which in its current form really isn't very useful, at least gives you an idea of what you are up against. Programming isn't much more complicated than the above lesson would indicate; there's just more to it. Now, if you plan on becoming an expert programmer who will set the world afire with revolutionary new applications for the computer, it's going to take a lot of study and practice. Good creative programmers spend years learning all the nuances of their trade. However, with just a few basic programming skills you can learn to create your own simple programs, and, what is even more important, you can modify existing programs that you buy on cassette tape.

The Power of Programming

To illustrate some of the interesting aspects of programming and its potential power, let's modify our loan program to see if we can't make it more useful.

As you may recall, when we entered the *RUN* command into the computer, it displayed the answer while part of the program ran off the top of the screen. If we want to take another look at the program, we can do so simply by using the BASIC command, *LIST*. By entering LIST, the program will reappear on the screen:

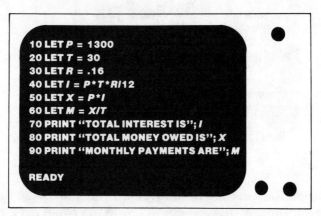

```
10 LET P = 1300
20 LET T = 30
30 LET R = .16
40 LET I = P*T*R/12
50 LET X = P*I
60 LET M = X/T
70 PRINT "TOTAL INTEREST IS"; I
80 PRINT "TOTAL MONEY OWED IS"; X
90 PRINT "MONTHLY PAYMENTS ARE"; M

READY
```

Let's say that you now want to find the interest, money owed, and monthly payments for a loan of $2400 at 18 percent for a period of 15 months. One way to do this would be to reenter lines 10, 20, and 30:

```
10 LET P = 2400
20 LET T = 15
30 LET R = .18
```

The computer will automatically replace the old entries with the new ones. Enter *RUN,* and the answers to this problem will appear:

```
TOTAL INTEREST IS 540
TOTAL MONEY OWED IS 2940
MONTHLY PAYMENTS ARE 196
```

Suppose we made an error and instead of entering 30 LET R = .18, we entered 30 LEET R = .18. In this case, when we enter *RUN* the computer will respond with:

```
WHAT?
30 L?EET R = .18
```

BASIC language lets you know when you have made an error and where the error occurred. In Radio Shack BASIC there are two error messages: WHAT? and HOW? WHAT? means the computer does not understand the instruction. This is caused by a misspelling, improper syntax, or punctuation error. HOW? means the computer understands the instruction, but can't execute it. This is usually because of something you forgot such as directing the computer to go to a certain line number and leaving the line number out of the instruction. Different BASICs have even more detailed error messages. Some of them will tell you when you've made a mistake only after you enter the RUN command (such as in the above example) while other BASICs will give you an error message immediately upon entering the improper program instructions. To correct the above mistake, we simply reenter the corrected statement:

```
30 LET R = .18
```

Editing the example program every time you want to solve a different loan problem could be boring. Suppose you are a neighborhood loan shark and you figure up to 100 such loans per day. By replacing the first three *LET* statements in this program with *INPUT* statements, we can make the program universal:

10 INPUT "AMOUNT OF LOAN"; P
20 INPUT "NUMBER OF MONTHS"; T
30 INPUT "RATE OF INTEREST"; R

Now, when we enter *RUN,* the computer responds with:

AMOUNT OF LOAN?

Let's say we enter $4800. The computer will then say:

NUMBER OF MONTHS:

Just for fun, we enter 48, and the computer comes back with:

RATE OF INTEREST?

We answer that our interest is .24 and the answers to the problem are immediately displayed:

TOTAL INTEREST IS 4608
MONEY OWED IS 9408
MONTHLY PAYMENTS ARE 196

Next, we can store this program on cassette tape so that we can load it into the computer and use it anytime we want. On a TRS-80 computer, all you have to do is insert a blank tape into the recorder, press the PLAY and RECORD buttons, enter CSAVE on the keyboard, and hit the ENTER key. The tape recorder will automatically be turned on and the program transferred to the tape for permanent storage. Once the program is loaded on the tape, the tape recorder will automatically turn off. By using the counter on the cassette tape recorder and indexing where on the tape you have stored programs, you can, of course, store more than one program on a tape. A good idea is to store each program twice in case you accidentally press the RECORD button.

As you use BASIC, you will learn more commands and instructions and you will learn new programming techniques. By using a feature of Radio Shack BASIC (also found on Microsoft BASIC) called *multiple statements per line* and by using abbreviations for commands and statements (which the computer will recognize), you can edit our sample program to look like this:

10 IN. "AMOUNT OF LOAN"; P:IN. "MONTHS"; T:IN.
   "RATE"; R
20 I = P*T*R/12:X = P + I:M = X/T
30 P. "TOTAL INTEREST"; I:P. "MONEY OWED"; X:P.
   "PAYMENTS"; M

The fun you can have programming your own computer and the satisfaction you'll receive is endless. In fact, why not put this book down right now, run to the nearest Radio Shack store or retail computer store, and try out our sample program. Computing is something you can learn best by doing.

6

A BUYER'S GUIDE TO PERSONAL COMPUTERS

Personal computers are really still in their infancy. Like automobiles, televisions, stereos, and other highly technical consumer products, it takes years before the dust settles in a new marketplace. Starting with the Altair in January 1975, at least 100 different personal computers have been introduced. Some of these computers are innovative and establish design ideas that will be around for years, while others are inferior, awkward products put out by people hoping to capitalize on what has been, up to now, a sellers' market. It seems that you can't go wrong by getting into the personal computing business, and indeed many people seem to have success almost in spite of themselves. Several of the major companies now in the business began as garage-shop operations, two or three friends getting together after work, tinkering around with electronic gear, coming up with something different, and then deciding to sell it.

Because personal computers require much more support than other consumer products, it is likely that the "cottage industry" aspects of the market will continue for years to come. However, as more established companies like Tandy Corporation (the Radio Shack people), Heath, Texas Instruments, etc., get into personal computing, it will become increasingly difficult, if not impossible, for garage-shop operators to grow up into major companies.

Since one of the thrusts of personal computing is increased personal freedom and power, it is hoped that many small companies will be able to use the personal computers they manufacture to stay in business when the competition gets rough. At one time there were over a hundred different companies manufacturing automobiles, yet now only a few are left. Many small companies in personal computing will probably turn away from manufacturing complete computer systems to manufacture instead specialized support products, such as line printers, terminals, floppy disks, and so on.

The buyer's guide to personal computers that appears in this chapter is intended to give you an idea of what's available and what to look for. Since the market is developing fast, some of the computers mentioned here will have been upgraded or may very well not even exist by the time you read this book. The intention of this guide, then, is to help you make more intelligent decisions if you do decide to buy a personal computer. It is a starting point. Many fine personal computers and related equipment will not even appear here because of limited space.

The Altair 8800b

This computer, manufactured by Mits/Pertec, is an updated version of the original Altair computer. Built around the Intel 8080 microprocessor, it is essentially a box-shaped computer, a little bigger than a typical stereo amplifier.

The first thing you'll probably notice about the Altair computer is all the lights and switches on its front panel. These switches and lights allow you to program the Altair in machine language, actually entering binary codes in the machine. In some versions of the Altair it is necessary that you do some of this, even though you might have a typewriter-style keyboard interfaced to the Altair. Before you can program some Altair systems in English-type instructions with your keyboard, you have to load its "programming language" into the

The Altair 8800b is an updated version of the original Altair. (*Courtesy Pertec Computer Corporation*)

machine using a series of binary codes (see chapter 2). This process is referred to as "bootstrap" loading of the machine. Once this is done, you needn't worry about the front panel lights and switches unless you really want to get into the fundamentals of computing. Personally, I find bootstrap loading to be cumbersome, and I tend to avoid it. But this complication can be avoided if the Altair is interfaced to a floppy disk system. It could also be avoided if Mits would put the programming language on a ROM (read only memory) chip. One final solution is to have a technical friend or a clerk at a computer store load the programming language in the Altair for you and then never turn the thing off and hope that you don't have a brownout in your neighborhood.

Aside from this technical problem, the Altair 8800b is a very well-supported, versatile computer. If you take the lid off the top of a basic Altair, you'll find that there is one circuit board inside the front panel, two circuit boards standing perpendicular to the front panel, and *16 empty slots where other circuit boards can be plugged into the machine.* These empty slots are called the *Altair BUS* or the *S-100 bus* system. There are over 100 different circuit boards that you can buy as options to plug into this bus.

Because it can be so readily expanded and adapted to many different applications, the Altair computer is called an open-ended computer. The circuit boards that can be plugged into it include memory boards, interface boards, and a wide variety of special application boards. One board, called an A to D Converter, allows you to interface the Altair to an electric device using analog signals* as opposed to the digital signals used by the computer. People are using their Altairs to control model railroads, stereos, burglar alarms, industrial machines, robots, and many other devices.

The Altair has been on the market long enough to have been tested in many areas. Floppy disks and hard disk memory systems have been successfully interfaced to the Altair along with line printers and a host of other peripherals. Software has been written for the Altair that makes it readily adaptable to both the business and home environment.

One drawback to the Altair, as far as beginners are concerned, is cost. The Altair 8800b without any memory sells for about $2000. Once you have added memory and interface boards and connected your Altair to the peripherals you need, you're talking about $5000 to $10,000. For many business uses, this is really very economical when compared to minicomputers; but for use as a home computer or a computer to learn on, the Altair is expensive.

The Sol Terminal Computer

Like the Altair, the Sol from Processor Technology is an S-100, open-ended computer built around the Intel 8080 microprocessor. The one immediately apparent difference between a Sol and an Altair is that the Sol has a built-in keyboard. It looks very much like an oversized typewriter.

Computer keyboards, like all other computer hardware, vary from one system to the next. One of the really nice features of the Sol is its keyboard. Many computer keyboards

---

*In an analog system, information is coded according to voltage rather than by the presence or absence of a current, as in a digital system.

The Sol Terminal Computer is pictured here with a Helios II floppy disk drive and video monitor. (*Courtesy Processor Technology, Inc.*)

only allow you to enter data and programs into the computer in upper-case characters. The Sol keyboard not only uses both upper and lower case, but it has a number of extra keys not found on many others. These include a "scratch pad" keyboard that fits alongside the regular, typewriter format keyboard. This scratch pad is a number and math function keyboard exactly like the ones on calculators and adding machines. Thus, with the Sol you can easily work problems involving numbers. Other keys on the Sol that you won't find on your standard typewriter keyboard include cursor control keys that allow you to move around the screen (assuming your Sol is hooked up to a television screen) so that you can easily edit programs and data. This makes the Sol a particularly nice computer for the word processing type applications we discussed earlier.

The Sol doesn't have as many slots (it has a total of 9) on its S-100 bus as an Altair does, but it doesn't need as many. Already built into the main board, which rests on the bottom of the case, are two interface *ports*, which allow you to hook up peripherals to the Sol without adding an interface board to the system as you have to do with an Altair. Also, when the Altair was originally introduced to the market, the only memory boards available that were compatible with an S-100 bus were 4K memory boards. Today, there are several companies, including Processor Technology and Mits, who produce 16K memory boards; and at least one company, IMS Associates, produces a 65K memory board.

Like the Altair, the Sol is priced in the neighborhood of $2000 (different accessories make this vary somewhat) and it is a little expensive for beginners. However, it too has been interfaced to a number of devices, including a Processor Technology floppy disk system. The software supporting the Sol is not as complete as that supporting the Altair. At the time of this writing, Processor Technology's BASIC left much to be desired. However, the longer this machine is in the field, the more complete it will become.

By the way, when computer people talk about businesses and people who actually use computers, they refer to us as *end-users*. Compared to insiders, we are computer-ignorant, which explains why they think we all live in the field. Letting us use computers and computer programs is called field testing.

The Tandy TRS-80

At the time of this writing, the TRS-80 or the Radio Shack Computer, as it is commonly called, is one of the best computers for a beginner to buy. Compared to most other computers, it is easier to use, less complicated, and probably one of the most reliable.

The basic TRS-80 consists of a keyboard, TV monitor, cassette recorder, AC power pack, user's manual, and two cassette tapes, one blank and the other containing two prerecorded games (blackjack and backgammon). It is built around the Z-80 microprocessor and comes with 4K of RAM memory plus 4K of ROM memory. The ROM memory contains the programming language, so you don't have to load it before you start using the computer.

It just happened that the TRS-80 computer that I have been using arrived at my office at the same time a film crew from one of the local television stations was filming an interview for a news special on personal computing. While the camera was rolling, we opened the box, read the easy-to-follow instructions for plugging the computer together, turned it on, and immediately began using it. We were ecstatic, and it made a good take.

Afterwards, the reporter asked me why I was so excited that the computer worked right off the bat. I explained to him that my past experience with computers had often been frustrating and time consuming. Usually, it was impossible to follow the instructions for setting up the machine, and then there were always problems loading the programming language. A personal computer system I once tried out for a review in *Personal Computing* magazine proved to be one of the most irritating experiences I've had with computers. I had three different technicians working on the computer, twice

The keyboard of the Tandy TRS-80 is functional, but it doesn't have many of the features found on a Sol keyboard, such as upper and lower-case characters and a calculator style scratchpad. (*Courtesy Radio Shack*)

sending memory boards back to the company, and when I finally gave up, I sent back the whole machine, which they promised to fix and return to me. I haven't heard from them since.

Aside from the machine itself, the most impressive aspect of the TRS-80 is the amount of support given it by Tandy Corporation. At the time the TRS-80 first came out, you could already buy inexpensive software application packages containing programs for your home or business. These application packages consist of eight cassette tapes cleverly packaged in the back of a three-ring binder. The instructions for using the tapes are on printed pages inside the binder. One of the packages is called a personal finance package and contains programs for balancing your checkbook and for keeping a monthly household budget. The other package that I personally have examined contains programs for keeping track of payroll for a small business. Tandy is one of the few companies to realize that applications are the key to selling computers to consumers. One imagines that in the near future, the local Radio Shack store will carry literally thousands of programmed cassette tapes for the TRS-80, making it a truly useful machine for home or small business. And you don't have to know a thing about programming to use these packages. Simply follow the easy instructions for loading the programs into the computer via cassette tape.

The keyboard on the TRS-80 is not nearly as impressive as the keyboard on the Sol computer. It doesn't have a scratch pad, upper and lower case characters, or some of the special function keys. However, it is quite adequate for many applications, and the feel of the keyboard is nice. (Just as with typewriters, computer keyboards vary considerably. Some of them have smooth action and are easy to use and some of them are sluggish and a pain in the neck.)

The television screen is a black and white monitor, and this limits some of the graphic fun you can have, but the TRS-80 can easily be programmed to make patterns, graphics, and pretty pictures. Aside from that, the screen has fairly good resolution, the letters show up quite nicely, and you can control the brightness. One note of caution here. The television provided with this computer has all its tuning circuitry removed, so if you were hoping to also use it as a TV, you're out of luck.

Internally, the TRS-80's memory can be expanded from 4K to 16K of memory simply by sending it back to the factory or returning it to one of the new Tandy Computer Centers (different from a Radio Shack). While the heat problems I mentioned earlier come into play when you expand a TRS-80 from 4K to 16K, it is my understanding that Radio Shack is working to correct this. Compared to the problems that many companies have with their computers when they are first field tested, this is relatively minor.

Another example of the fine support Radio Shack gives its customers is the user's manual that comes with a TRS-80. This manual includes a BASIC programming course that is one of the finest I've ever run across, and it lets you learn while you are using the computer. Aside from applications, literature is really the key to the consumer computer business. Many companies have fancy, powerful computers but don't know how to explain to the public what they are or how they work. For instance, here are a few sentences from a brochure on the microNOVA computer from Data General:

> The microNOVA mN601 microprocessor is a NOVA CPU in a single 40-pin ceramic package. 16-bit data paths and multiple-register architecture provide data precision and efficient storage of intermediate results.*

Having read this book, you should know what some of that jargon means (CPU and microprocessor), but can you imagine trying to make up your mind to buy one if you are a small businessman?

As for expansion of a TRS-80 computer, it is not an S-100 bus computer like the Altair and Sol computers. Memory expansion to 16K is accomplished by plugging additional memory chips into the single circuit board that fits on the bottom of

*Data General microNOVA brochure. Copyright© 1976 by Data General Corporation.

the keyboard case. This circuit card contains the microprocessor, support circuitry, memory chips, and interface chips. The Radio Shack computer is referred to as a *single-board* computer. This makes it much more economical than S-100 computers (retail price is just $598), but more difficult to expand and add peripherals to.

Radio Shack's solution to this problem rests in a flip-top door about 2 inches long and 1/2 inch wide located on the upper left corner of the keyboard. Inside this door is a 40-pin connector (a plug, like a wall plug only with 40 prongs instead of the traditional 2 or 3). Just available at the time of this writing from Radio Shack is an expansion box that plugs into this 40-pin connector. This box, which is designed to fit underneath the TV screen, is a bus system that will allow you to add circuit boards to the TRS-80 and thus interface it to peripherals such as line printers and floppy disks.

VideoBrain

Many high-technology manufacturers will be able to build the necessary hardware for personal computers, but the real revolution in consumers' acceptance of computers will come in providing a total hardware and software package that fully utilizes the computer's power while making it immediately accessible.

—Richard Melmon
Vice President, Marketing
VideoBrain Computer Co.

VideoBrain Computer Company is a newly formed company with some high-powered personnel and bold ideas. Richard Melmon, who is quoted above, directed the introduction of the first mass marketed LCD digital watch for Microma and, prior to that, did strategic market planning for companies like Intel, Hewlett-Packard, and Monsanto. The president of the company, Dr. Albert Yu, directed the technology and product development at Intel Corporation for five years, and the vice-president, Dr. David Chung, was the inventor and program director of the Fairchild F-8 microprocessor (which just happens to be the CPU of the VideoBrain). Apparently these gentlemen got tired of working for sleeping electronic giants and decided to go out into the world and wake people up to the home computer.

One major question about the VideoBrain computer is: *Is it really a computer?* In my opinion, the answer is no. The VideoBrain is really a sophisticated video game, one with a keyboard and some practical programs, but it isn't a computer because it can't be programmed by the user. If you want to modify the programs that you buy from VideoBrain or if you want to write your own programs, you are out of luck. However, VideoBrain could easily *become* a computer and there are some exciting programs available for it that make it worth talking about.

The VideoBrain Computer is programmed with plug-in cartridges like programmable video games. (*Courtesy VideoBrain Computer Company*)

The VideoBrain is basically a black box with a built-in keyboard that connects to a television set. It can operate in both color and black and white, and it is programmed with the same kind of ROM cartridges used to program the Fairchild video game. The VideoBrain is scheduled to sell for under $500, and the cartridges for $19.95.

According to company literature, the VideoBrain can be expanded by using optional expanders for interfacing to a tape cassette player, line printer, or telephone modem (a device for interfacing the computer to a telephone so that computer data can be sent over telephone lines). If VideoBrain is expanded into this area, it seems to me that programming capability will have to be added to it and then it will quit being a sophisticated video game and become a real computer.

But then, what difference does it make if the VideoBrain is a computer or a game? The distinction will be understood by those who are familiar with computers, but probably won't be understood by the general public. The principals of Video-Brain are correct about one thing: *People don't care so much about what it is as long as it does what they want it to.* In this regard, VideoBrain is a giant step forward in the personal computing business.

According to VideoBrain literature, there will soon be over 50 cassette cartridges available for the VideoBrain. It is in this area where VideoBrain is significant. At the time of the introduction of the VideoBrain there were already 12 of these available, including the following.

FINANCE I

A program for "sophisticated" analysis of loans, mortgages, savings accounts, and other financial alternatives. Computes net present value, internal rate of return, accumulated interest or principal for any period, interest rate or term of loan. The program will even graph the results of the last eight evaluations and will let the user write formulas for evaluation with up to 20 user-defined variables.

CASH MANAGEMENT I

Uses the cassette interface to record and summarize all household income and spending. You enter your transactions for a month and VideoBrain displays a summary of where your money came from, where it went, and how much you now have in each of your checking, savings, and other accounts. It will also keep track of credit cards and charge accounts.

REAL ESTATE ANALYSIS I

Will construct projected income and cash-flow statements for any piece of property you might be considering. You can evaluate the pretax and aftertax consequences of any contingency.

MUSIC TEACHER I

Teaches you how to read, write, and play music in a four-octave range. When you play a note on the VideoBrain keyboard, the note is played through the TV, and the note is named and displayed in five-line musical notation on the screen. Once you've played a tune, the VideoBrain will play it back just as you keyed it in. The program includes two built-in songs that it will teach you. When you've learned to read music, you can use the VideoBrain as a musical instrument to play any written melody.

WORDWISE I

This program trains one to four people in word-building skills at three different skill levels. The VideoBrain gives each person a random assortment of ten letters and challenges the person to build words with them. The program includes a challenge round (to correct score for misspelled words) and a song to salute the best word builder.

WORDWISE II

Wordwise II teaches accurate touch typing through three exercises. VideoBrain signals your mistakes and records your progress with a words-per-minute score after every exercise.

Most of the other programs available for VideoBrain at the time of this writing were game programs similar to the ones found with other video game units. It seems to me that the approach of VideoBrain is very exciting. It is a worthwhile "computer" to keep your eyes on.

The Apple II Computer

Considered by many to be the "Cadillac" of home computers, the Apple II computer has many technical advances and features not found on other personal computers. Consisting of a keyboard in a single plastic case, the Apple does not come with a TV monitor like the TRS-80. However, it can be connected to any television set by using an inexpensive RF modulator, available at most television repair shops. While on the surface this may seem to be a drawback to the Apple, it isn't because the Apple has been designed for use with a home *color* television. Special software that comes with the machine allows you to produce dazzling graphics and color displays in either one of two modes, *color graphics* or *high-resolution graphics*.

In the color graphics mode the resolution of the screen is 40 lines wide by 48 high, and you have a choice of 15 colors to work with. In the high-resolution mode you have only four colors, but the screen is divided into 280 lines wide by 192 high. Each of these modes allows you four lines of alphanumeric characters at the bottom of the screen so you can label graphics, give some instructions, or have the computer ask you questions.

In many ways, the approach of Apple has been revolutionary and has shown some real foresight on the part of the engineers who started the company. Apple was founded in January 1975, by Steven Jobs and Stephen Wozniak. In less than two years it was out of the garage where it started and into its 20,000-square-foot international headquarters in Cupertino, California. Aside from technical excellence, Apple's success has been founded on its careful marketing strategy and consumer orientation. Unlike many companies founded by technical people, Apple has not let its technical expertise overshadow its marketing efforts. Chairman of the Board and Vice-President of Marketing Chuck Markkula spent many years in key marketing positions with Intel, Fairchild, and Hughes Aircraft before moving over to Apple. Included with the Apple II are two paddles similar to the ones found on

Many people consider the Apple II Computer to be the "Cadillac" of home computers. (*Courtesy Apple, Inc.*)

home video games. These paddles, combined with the color graphics and a built-in speaker for sound effects, allow you to play a wide variety of TV games including Pong™*, tank, and many others. In fact, with an Apple, you'll soon be writing your own video games.

The programming language for the Apple which includes special graphic functions is on ROM so you don't have to worry about loading, and the machine is capable of being expanded to 48K of memory (the basic unit comes with 8K) simply by adding more memory chips to its single circuit board. It is built around the 6502 microprocessor chip.

Apple tries to combine the best features of a single-board computer with those of a bus system type computer. Built into the main board, which rests on the bottom of the case, is a cassette tape interface for external memory storage. Unlike the

*Pong is a trademark of Atari.

TRS-80, the Apple will not require an expansion box to interface it to peripheral devices. On the back of the main board are 8 peripheral board connectors that allow you to plug miniature circuit cards into the Apple in much the same way as you plug circuit cards into an Altair or a Sol. The system isn't nearly as versatile as the S-100 or Altair bus system, and at the time of this writing, Apple was the only company making boards available for it, but it gives Apple a running head start over Radio Shack and other single-board computers. Boards available for this "mini-bus" at the time of writing included a line printer interface, a wireless remote AC controller for controlling appliances in your home, a music synthesizer, and a voice recognition system. Other boards soon to be announced by Apple include a floppy disk controller board and an RS-232 interface board, which can be used to hook the Apple up to a number of different peripherals.

By using high density components and many design innovations, the engineers at Apple were able to design the Apple II with one-quarter to one-third the number of parts used in some other personal computers. Thus, the Apple is light in weight and easy to handle. Also, with fewer parts, the chances of failure are reduced considerably, and over the years the Apple II should prove to be one of the most reliable personal computers.

In its basic configuration, the Apple II comes with 8K of RAM memory (expandable to 48K) and 8K of ROM on which the programming language (BASIC) is stored along with a system monitor. Application software available for the Apple include a checkbook balancing program, basic home finance program, education programs, and games. There is also a users group open to all Apple owners called the Apple Software Bank that serves as a vehicle for exchanging information and programs with other Apple owners.

Where Apple is weak compared to Radio Shack is in price and support. At the time of this writing, the Apple II sold for about $1400. Apple simply doesn't have the resources that Tandy Corporation has and therefore can't build up its production as fast or provide the amount of software support.

Still, the product is very good and is having a significant impact on the personal computing market. Time will tell if Apple will be able to put it all together and stay competitive.

The Renaissance Machine

As the personal computing market develops, we will undoubtedly see more features built into personal computers and less need to interface them to external devices. A step in this direction is provided by Compucolor Corporation of Norcoss, Georgia, with its newly announced Renaissance Machine, also known as Compucolor II. Like the Apple II, the Renaissance Machine has been designed to work with a color TV monitor, which is provided as part of an interesting package.

The basic Renaissance Machine includes a separate keyboard (as is the case with the TRS-80) and a color TV monitor with built-in mini disk drive. It is this built-in disk drive (for miniature floppy disks) that makes the Renaissance different from any other personal computer. Unlike cassette tape memory storage, programs on a floppy disk can be "formatted" into separate files for instant access. The speed and ease of use of floppy disks over cassette tape is remarkable. To store a program on a floppy disk, you enter the word *SAVE* plus an arbitrary name for the program (such as BUDGET), and the computer will instantly store the program on the disk. To reenter the program, you enter LOAD BUDGET and the program is instantly put back into the computer's memory. By entering DIRECTORY, the computer will output a list of the programs or files stored on the disk. These and other features make floppy disk storage the wave of the future. Personal computers in the 1980s will probably not use cassette tape.

The Renaissance Machine comes with a whopping 16K of ROM that can be expanded to 32K. This Read Only Memory contains an advanced BASIC programming language that includes 13 commands for working with the floppy disk drive, and it also contains software necessary for text editing features like the ability to erase a page or line, tab, and page roll (so that information isn't lost when a line goes off the bottom of the screen).

The Renaissance Machine from Compucolor Corporation includes a color monitor with a built-in mini floppy drive. (*Courtesy Compucolor Corporation*)

In addition to the ROM memory, the basic unit comes with 8K of RAM memory that is expandable to 24K. Some of this user memory is used by the machine itself to "refresh" the color monitor (4K in the 8K version and 8K in the 24K version).

Each floppy disk stores 50 to 60K bytes of memory, depending on how the memory is formatted. Another nice feature is the capability to transfer data from the disk to the computer or from the computer to an optional line printer and vice versa at one of 14 user-selectable speeds.

Programs available from Compucolor include a variety of games written to take advantage of the color graphics, plus a payroll program, recipe and menu program, checkbook program, and math tutor program.

At the time of this writing, the Compucolor II wasn't being delivered yet, though it had been demonstrated at a couple of trade shows. There are many questions remaining about performance, support, and reliability, but the product idea is very sound, and one would hope the company will be able to back it up.

The Heathkit H8 Computer

For people who are into building their own electronic kits, Heathkit's new H8 Computer is highly recommended. Heath has a long history of manufacturing electronic kits and is currently the largest company in this business. Heath offers nearly 400 electronic kits of virtually every description.

The main advantage of a Heathkit is its documentation. Heath knows better than anyone how to write instructions for building and operating electronic products. This comes from years of experience and testing. If you are inexperienced at kit building, you can probably build a Heathkit computer without too much difficulty (it will take some time, however). Building a kit from some of the other manufacturers is impossible unless you have a great deal of experience and know how to read schematic diagrams.

Like the Altair and Sol computers, the Heathkit H8 is an open-ended computer built around the 8080 microprocessor. Unlike these two machines, the Heath computer does not have an S-100 bus structure so that the wide variety of S-100 circuit boards on today's market are not compatible with the H8. This has caused some controversy, particularly among hobbyists who were hoping that Heath would manufacture an S-100 machine. Heath's answer to this criticism is that the S-100 bus has never really been well defined and that it is too expensive. There is some truth to these points. The manufacturers of S-100 computers and S-100 circuit boards have never gotten together to standardize the S-100 bus, thus some S-100 products are not truly compatible with others. If you do buy an S-100 computer, you will have to be careful about how you expand it. One way to assure compatibility is always to buy circuit cards from the same company that made the computer. Another way is to verify with a knowledgeable friend or a

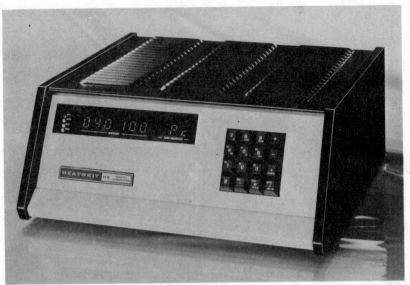

The Heathkit H8 Computer (*Courtesy Heath Company*)

computer retailer that the circuit board you want to add to your computer is compatible; that others have successfully used the same combination you wish to use.

In any case, the H8 computer can be expanded like the Altair and the Sol. The basic unit, which sold for $375 at the time of this writing, comes with a front panel circuit board and a CPU circuit board with room to add an additional 9 boards. In order for the H8 to be useful at all, you have to buy a memory board. Heath offers a 4K memory board kit that is expandable to 8K for $140. To expand it to 8K, you simply plug in additional memory chips, which are available from Heath for $95. Thus, an H8 computer with 8K of memory currently sells for $610.

The one, immediately apparent difference between a Heathkit H8 computer and an Altair computer is the front panel. Instead of having rows of toggle switches and LED lights, the H8 front panel consists of a scratch pad style keyboard and a large LED readout panel. To program the H8 in machine language , you enter instructions in *octal* instead of binary. Octal is a base-8 number system that is easier and somewhat faster to use than binary numbers. A ROM chip inside the H8 converts octal numbers to binary numbers that the computer can understand. Of course, this is only useful if you really want to get into computers and understand their basic operation. If you want to program the Heathkit computer in BASIC, then you will first have to interface it to a computer terminal. When Heath announced the H8 computer, it also announced the availability of a CRT terminal (essentially a TV screen with a typewriter-style keyboard) and a keyboard printer terminal (essentially a line printer with a keyboard). These products can be connected to the H8 to make it a really

The Heathkit H9 video terminal is an input/output peripheral designed to be interfaced with the Heath H8 Computer. (*Courtesy Heath Company*)

powerful system. You can also add a cassette recorder or a paper tape reader to the H8 for program loading and storage (external memory).

While the Heath bus system is somewhat cheaper than an S-100 bus system, it is still quite a bit more expensive than a single-board computer. To give you an idea of this expense, look at the following comparison of the cost of H8 with all the options needed to program it in BASIC with a Radio Shack computer:

Radio Shack TRS-80	*Health H8 Computer System*	
(Completely assembled with built-in keyboard, TV screen, and cassette recorder, including 4K memory and the programming language on ROM memory chips.)	Basic H8 kit	$ 375.00
	4K memory kit	140.00
	Interface board	110.00
	TV terminal	530.00
	Cassette recorder	55.00
Cost: $598.00		Cost: $1,210.00

(Includes programming language on cassette tape that has to be loaded into machine and thus uses up much of the 4K internal memory.)

The result is $1210 for a kit you have to build yourself compared to $598 for a computer that is ready to go. Of course, the advantage of the H8 at the time of this writing is that it is easier to expand. For a beginner who really wants to understand the hows and whys of computers, the Heathkit might be the way to go. However, for the beginner who wants to understand only how to use a computer, the Radio Shack TRS-80 clearly has the upper hand.

Before we leave the Heathkit, we should mention that Heath also manufactures another computer, the H11, which is considerably more powerful (and more expensive) than the H8.

The H11 kit computer, which sold for $1295 at the time of this writing, is a 16-bit machine as opposed to an 8-bit

The Heathkit Hll Computer uses 16-bit bytes as compared to the 8-bit bytes used in most personal computers. (*Courtesy Heath Company*)

machine. This means that every byte of information processed by the H11 is in the form of 16 binary numbers instead of 8 binary numbers. Thus, the H11 is both more powerful and faster than 8-bit machines. Also, the CPU of the H11 computer is the same as the CPU of the PDP-11 computer from Digital Equipment Corporation, which is probably the most popular minicomputer on the market. This means that the software that has been written for the PDP-11 (and there is literally tons of it) is compatible with the H11 from Heath. PDP-11 computers are really too expensive to be considered personal computers, but if you are interested in a very powerful business computer, the H11 is certainly worth looking into.

The PET Computer

The PET computer from Commodore (a company that manufactures calculators and digital watches) was the first complete low-cost personal computer to be announced. However, because of Commodore's production problems, the Radio Shack TRS-80 was actually the first computer of this type to be delivered to customers.

Like the TRS-80, the basic PET comes complete with 4K of memory, a programming language (BASIC) on ROM, built-in cassette recorder, TV screen, and keyboard. Unlike the TRS-80, all of these parts are housed in a single cabinet.

Built around the 6502 microprocessor (as is the Apple computer), the PET has a number of advantages and disadvantages when compared to the Radio Shack computer. Pricewise it sells for $595, which makes it actually $3 cheaper than a basic TRS-80.

The number one disadvantage of a PET computer is its keyboard. It is a small (very small) keyboard that is completely flat. Unlike most standard keyboards, the rows of keys are not staggered, and thus they don't have the same feel that a typewriter keyboard has. The special characters are scattered about in defiance of usual conventions, and if you wish to use upper and lower case, you have to get used to shifting for lower case (there is no shift lock, so you can imagine what a chore this could become in a word processing application). However, included on the keyboard are special graphics characters that make the PET a lot of fun if you want to draw pictures and charts.

At the time of this writing, the major advantage of the PET over the TRS-80 is its BASIC. Written by a company called Microsoft, this language has many extra features and is a lot faster than the Radio Shack language.

Also, the PET could prove to be somewhat easier to expand than the Radio Shack computer. Its internal memory can only be expanded from 4K to 8K instead of from 4K to 16K as with the Radio Shack, but Commodore does provide two standard interface plugs on the back of the PET that may be interfaced with a line printer. The advantage of having two cassette recorders hooked up to a computer instead of one is similar to the advantage of having two tape drives instead of one on a stereo system. You can swap information from one cassette to another. One could be used to store programs and the other could be used to store data. Additional expansion of the PET will have to be accomplished the same way TRS-80 expansion is accomplished—that is, with an external box. At the time of this writing, no such box was yet available for the PET.

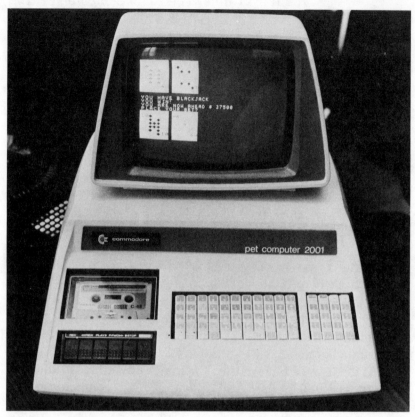

The PET Computer (*Courtesy Commodore Business Machines, Inc.*)

One advantage the Radio Shack computer would seem to have over the PET is in the area of support. Tandy Corporation (the corporate owners of Radio Shack stores) have a broad, worldwide distribution system already set up with more than 8000 participating stores. Also, they have been very fast in providing good literature and application programs for their computer. Commodore doesn't seem to have these same resources and doesn't seem to be able to support their computer the way Radio Shack does. However, this could change rapidly if Commodore is successful in its negotiations with Sears, Montgomery Ward, Macy's, and other department stores. These chains have expressed some interest in the PET computer and they could provide Commodore with a lot of marketing muscle and, presumably, cash to support their computer products. Sears did announce in the fall of 1977 that they would be test marketing the PET in selected stores, but apparently this plan fell through. The PET computer could conceivably become the most popular of personal computers and undoubtedly it will be used by thousands of people.

The Noval 760 Computer

Talk about class. The Noval 760 computer from Noval, Incorporated, is a beautiful computer system that comes completely encased in handsome rosewood. For $3385 you get a Z-80 based computer with 32K of external memory plus some special memory features on ROM, a video screen, full

The Noval 760 Computer (*Courtesy Noval Incorporated*)

keyboard, digital cassette tape recorder, speaker, and three additional interface ports. The digital cassette tape recorder is a special tape recorder made for computers that records the digital information on tape instead of recording the audio equivalents of this information.

Actually, the Noval is out of the price range of most beginners, but for a small business system it is very economically priced when you consider all of its features.

Other Computers

This discussion of personal computers shouldn't serve as your sole guide when buying a computer. There are many other computers on the market besides the ones mentioned here. Digital Group, an engineering company in Denver, Colorado, manufactures a complete line of personal computers and related peripherals that many people will swear by (including the Neiman-Marcus department stores, which sell a Digital Group system under their own name). APF, one of the major companies in the video game business, recently announced a computer they call the PECOS that has a unique programming language which the company claims is easier to use and more powerful than the programming languages found on other personal computers. Cromemco, one of the pioneer companies in the personal computing business, manufactures some rugged computer gear that has been very successful in the educational and industrial markets as well as in the personal computing market. IMSAI manufactures an improved version of the Altair computer, which at the time of this writing was outselling the Altair by at least two to one. Other companies manufacturing personal computers (see Appendix B) include E & L Instruments, Southwest Technical Products, North Star, Extensys, Parasitic Engineering,* Technical Design Labs, Ohio Scientific, Space Byte, Polymorphic,

---

*Parasitic Engineering got its name from an editorial written by Ed Roberts in the May 1975 issue of Mits' company publication, *Computer Notes.* In this editorial, Roberts likened companies that manufactured Altair-compatible and imitation Altair products to parasites. While it was a good joke at the time, my guess is that Parasitic Engineering will eventually change its name to something more sensible.

Vector Graphics, TLF, Ximedia, and Midwest Scientific Instruments. And we haven't even mentioned some of the minicomputer manufacturers who are selling business systems that are gradually getting inexpensive enough to be considered personal computers. These include Data General, Digital Equipment Corporation, Texas Instruments, and yes, even good old IBM.

Summary

The computers reviewed here were selected to give you an idea of the wide range of computers available and what some of the considerations should be if you decide to buy a computer. Buying a computer is much the same as buying a new car. There are many different manufacturers, dealers, and representatives, each selling that special computer that is clearly better than all the rest. From our discussion you know that some of the factors to look for are expandability, software support, applications, reliability, built-in features, under-

The Poly 88, an inexpensive S-100 computer, is just one example of the many fine personal computers available today. (*Courtesy Polymorphic Systems, Inc.*)

standability, and price. The Altair, Sol, and Heath computers are easily expandable. The Compucolor II has the most built-in features. The Apple, like the Compucolor, has dazzling color graphic capabilities, and it was designed with a great deal of foresight and technical excellence. The Radio Shack and PET give you more computer for the price than anyone else. Heath and Radio Shack provide the best documentation and seem to understand consumers better than most other companies. VideoBrain has its own unique approach which could prove to be a big winner in the home market. The Altair has good software support and has been successfully used for many applications. The Noval computer looks good and is an excellent system for small business applications. Because computers can be used in so many different ways, the proliferation of different kinds and styles of computers will probably go on and on. The number of companies may narrow down to a handful of major manufacturers, but these manufacturers, like GM and Ford, will offer many different models to choose from, and yes, there will be foreign competition. The Japanese, in particular, have made many advances in semiconductor technology, and literally hundreds of Japanese businessmen have attended one or more of the major personal computing shows held around the coutnry.

Before you buy a computer, do some careful shopping. Stop in at a retail store (see Appendix A), write letters to manufacturers asking for product literature, read about computers in the many hobby computer magazines that are available (see Appendix C), and talk to a friend or anyone who has purchased a personal computer to find out what their experiences have been. The amount of investigating and learning you can do prior to buying a computer is really unlimited. If, for example, you are interested in the Heathkit H8 computer, you can purchase from Heath a copy of the complete set of H8 documentation for $25.00. This literature, which comes in a three-ring binder, weighs eleven pounds. The price you pay for it can be deducted from the price of an H8 if you decide to buy one. Many other manufacturers offer similar arrangements.

7

A BUYER'S GUIDE TO COMPUTER PERIPHERALS

Computer peripherals are machines or devices that you interface or connect to your computer. As our discussion of computers clearly indicated, some computers require the addition of more peripherals to make them complete systems. While the Radio Shack TRS-80 already has a keyboard for inputting information, a video screen for outputting information, and a cassette recorder for external storage, many computers, such as the Altair and Heath H8, do not have these options built into their basic configuration. As with stereo systems, with computers you can go the "component route" or you can buy a complete unit with everything included.

Until the development of single-board computers with built-in peripherals, many personal computer users were surprised and even dismayed to find out that the cost of the peripherals can be greater than the cost of the computer. A high-quality TV terminal can run into thousands of dollars, as can high-quality line printers, floppy disks, and other devices. However, the need for low-cost peripheral devices and the attractive volume sales that are now possible have spurred many manufacturers into entering the low-cost peripheral market. Still, the price reductions in this area aren't likely to match the reduction in prices found in computers. The reason for this is that peripherals are built mostly from mechanical devices rather than electronic devices. The price reduction in computers has been brought about largely by the miniaturization and subsequent price drops in electronic components. Meanwhile, the prices of mechanical devices such as the printing mechanisms found in line printers have, in many cases, increased rather than decreased.

As we indicated earlier, peripherals are basically divided into three categories: (1) input devices (keyboards); (2) output devices (line printers); and (3) external memory storage devices (cassette recorders).

The following discussion of peripherals will be even more incomplete than our discussion of personal computers. The sheer number and variety of these devices are staggering. Listing them would take up an entire book. However, we can look at a few of them and develop some ideas about what their basic features are and what to look for if you decide to buy one, two, or a dozen. (It is theoretically possible to interface 256 peripherals to one single Altair computer.) Perhaps it is best to begin this section with the one peripheral that combines all of the above three functions.

The Teletype Machine

The most common input/output device used with early microcomputers was the ASR Teletype machine. This machine, which was in use long before computers, includes a typewriter-style keyboard, hardcopy output,* and a paper tape reader/punch for mass memory storage. Today over 1,000,000 Teletype machines have been manufactured, and hundreds of thousands of them are in common use today.

While the cost of a new Teletype machine is about $1500, many hobbyists have been able to buy used Teletypes for $250 or less. Also, they are relatively easy to interface to computers. One of the first circuit boards made for the S-100 Altair bus was a TTY interface board. If you plan on using a Teletype with your computer, you will need to make sure that a TTY in-

---

*Hardcopy is simply printed material in a permanent form that can be handled and stored. Information printed on a video monitor is not hardcopy.

terface port is either built into the machine or can be added as an option.

Many computer companies, including Heath and Mits, provide software on paper tape so that it can easily be entered into the computer via teletype or via a peripheral called a *paper tape reader*. The drawback to this method of mass storage is speed and data integrity. Loading the programming language into a microcomputer via paper tape through a

The Heathkit H10 Papertape Reader/Punch (*Courtesy Heath Company*)

Teletype machine can sometimes take as long as 20 minutes. Also, the paper tapes tend to get bent, so you have to be very careful how you handle them. It is always a good idea to make extra copies of the tapes in case you have an accident.

Reading paper tapes is not the only thing that is time consuming about a Teletype. Unfortunately, the keyboard is agonizingly slow and requires a great deal of patience if you are used to using an electric typewriter. The other drawback to this very versatile computer peripheral is noise. Teletypes tend to clatter a lot and you wouldn't want to have one in your living room. Unless your computer is set up in a place that is relatively isolated from other activity, a Teletype machine can be quite a nuisance.

One more thing that you should know about Teletype machines is that there are two other models available other than the ASR Teletype. A KSR Teletype is one without the paper tape reader and punch, and an RO Teletype is one that has no keyboard and can only be used as a printer.

The American Dream Machine

As microcomputers developed, many people started using video display terminals as input/output devices instead of Teletype machines. As you know from our discussion about various computers, many of the more recent, single-board computers have video display units built right in. Included in this category are the PET and TRS-80 microcomputers.

Video display terminals are faster than Teletype machines and they are quiet. Their main disadvantage is that they don't provide a permanent record (hardcopy).

Video display terminals are commonly referred to as CRT (cathode ray tube) terminals. The screen on your home television set is a cathode ray tube.

Perhaps the most common video display terminal found interfaced to microcomputers is the ADM-3A "dumb terminal" from Lear-Siegler, also known as the American Dream Machine. This terminal is referred to as a "dumb" terminal because it does not have a microprocessor chip built into it as

The ADM-3A Dumb Terminal is shown here with the Model 210 Ballistic Printer. (*Courtesy Lear-Siegler, Inc.*)

do some other video display terminals, which are referred to as "smart" terminals. These "smart" terminals, which can cost as much as $10,000, are often interfaced to maxicomputers. Some of the routine programming on these setups is done right in the terminal so as not to bother the computer, which assumedly has more important things to do. Also "smart" terminals, if they have enough internal memory, can be used as computers. The Radio Shack TRS-80 computer could be considered a "smart" terminal. In fact, many people have discussed the possibility of using a TRS-80 as a "smart" terminal interfaced to a larger computer.

The ADM-3A terminal provides you with 24 lines of 80-characters-per-line display. This is approximately the same amount of text found on a typewritten sheet of 8½-by-11-inch paper, double-spaced. Other terminals on the market do not provide this much text, which is a consideration you should keep in mind.

The ADM-3A can be interfaced to any computer with an RS-232 standard interface. There are many RS-232 interface boards available for the S-100 computers, and most other computers provide this as a standard option.

The keyboard of the basic ADM-3A does not include a scratch-pad keyboard in addition to the typewriter-style keyboard as does the keyboard on the Sol computer. Also, it does not have lower-case characters. However, these features are provided by Lear-Siegler as options. The last price I saw on an ADM-3A without these options was $1125 assembled. (You can also build one of these terminals from a kit and save about 10 percent on the cost.)

Two features not found on the ADM-3A which can be very useful (and expensive), are tabbing and scrolling. As with a typewriter, tabbing is the ability to set tabs with a tabulator key. Once this is done, the cursor will automatically jump to the next tab-stop position. Scrolling is a feature that lets you look at text that has more lines than the screen can display at one time. This is accomplished either by holding a limited amount of text in RAM memory inside the CRT terminal, or better yet by holding an unlimited amount of text both inside the CRT and outside in conjunction with a floppy disk. Scrolling and tabbing are two features that are very useful in text-editing applications.

Selecterm System 9710

Micro Computer Devices, a small company in Anaheim, California, is marketing an IBM Selectric II typewriter called the Selecterm that can be interfaced to any computer with a standard parallel or serial (RS-232) interface port. The words *parallel* and *serial* simply refer to the method in which data are transferred from the computer to the peripheral. When data are transferred serially, they are transferred one bit at a time; and when they are transferred in a parallel fashion, they are transferred one byte or 8 bits at a time. Obviously, the parallel method is faster than the serial method. Most personal computers have one or the other; many have both.

The main advantage in using an IBM Selectric over a line printer is the type. Most line printers use a dot matrix typeface, which means that each character (letter, number, or symbol) is a series of dots. If the line printer uses a 5-by-7-dot matrix, this means all the characters are constructed by using any one of a

The Selecterm is a fully converted IBM Selectric II Typewriter that can be interfaced to many personal computers. (*Courtesy Micro Computer Devices, Inc.*)

number of a combination of dots in a square that is 7 dots high by 5 dots wide that looks like this:

```
●●●●●
●0000
●0000
●●●●0
●0000
●0000
●●●●●
```

The characters are actually generated by a row of miniature hammers called printhammers that sweep across the paper making dots in the appropriate places by hitting the paper through an inked ribbon. While a 5-by-7-dot matrix is adequate for creating upper-case letters, it does a poor job with lower-case characters. A 5-by-9 dot matrix is much better, though more expensive. The time and temperature display seen at many banks uses dot matrix characters. Obviously, this typeface is not as aesthetically pleasing or as easy to read as standard typefaces. It looks like something that was done with a computer.

If you are interested in using a computer for writing letters, the Selecterm will do a very nice job. The letters you write will be personal and you can even change the typeface by changing the type ball that has made the IBM Selectric one of the most versatile typewriters on the market today. When writing promotional letters, it is always more effective to use a combination of standard type, italicized type, and boldface type.

Another advantage the Selecterm has over most line printers is the paper. It uses any paper that will fit into the carriage of the typewriter. Line printers generally use standard line printer paper that has a series of vertical holes running down both edges of the sheet. Also, line printer paper tends to be green with white horizontal stripes, which looks ugly but makes it easy to read columns of numbers. Of course, there are many special types of line printer paper available on the market today, but this is one of the considerations you should keep in mind if you decide you need hardcopy.

The main disadvantage of the Selecterm may be its price. At the time of this writing, it sold for $1650. Another question is whether it really can be interfaced to any computer as is claimed by Micro Computer Devices. Part of the package you buy is software in PROM that will handle the conversion of the computer output (the bits) into characters that the typewriter understands. Before I bought one of these, I'd make sure that it had already been successfully interfaced to the type of computer I wanted to interface it to. Your local computer retailer (see Appendix A) should be able to help you with this question.

Qume, Okidata, and Axiom

There are many line printers on the market, so in order to make the points clearly, I have limited this discussion to three printers that have different characteristics to illustrate some of the considerations.

The Okidata Model 110, which has been very popular

with personal computer users, is a 5-by-7-dot matrix printer (see page 117). It prints *bidirectionally* on an 8½-inch roll of paper, or if it has an optional "tractor feed," 9½-inch paper. One of the features and advantages of the Okidata is that it is an impact printer: Thus you can print up to three carbon copies when you use the 9½-inch format. At 110 characters per second or 65 lines per minute, the Okidata is fairly slow as impact printers go, but it is certainly fast enough for most home or small business applications. If you wanted to print 200,000 mailing address labels with this machine, it could take a long time compared to more expensive printers. Cost of this printer is approximately $1500.

The Axiom printer is an example of a nonimpact or thermal printer. Its characters are generated by passing a high current from fine wires in its print head to the surface of the paper. The paper, which is an electrosensitive or electrostatic paper, is coated with a fine layer of aluminum that dissolves instantly upon contact with the electric current, exposing a layer of black ink—the next layer of the paper. Like the Okidata, characters are formed out of a dot matrix, only this matrix is 5 by 8 instead of 5 by 7, giving lower-case characters a much better appearance. Also, you have the option of three sizes of characters, which can even be mixed on the same line.

Nonimpact printers are generally faster than impact printers, and the Axiom is no exception. The small-size characters are generated at 320 characters per second. Unlike the Okidata, the Axiom only prints in one direction, so some time (approximately one-quarter second) is lost for carriage return.

The disadvantage of the Axiom is the paper, which in addition to being specially coated (and thus more expensive) is only five inches wide. You wouldn't want to use this paper for sending computer letters, though it is fine for many record-keeping applications. Also, you can't make carbon copies with a thermal printer.

The advantages of the Axiom printer over the Okidata are speed, lack of noise, and price. While the Okidata makes quite a clattering sound, the Axiom hums very quietly and actually sounds rather dignified. It sells for approximately $700.

Qume Corporation is one of only two companies (the other

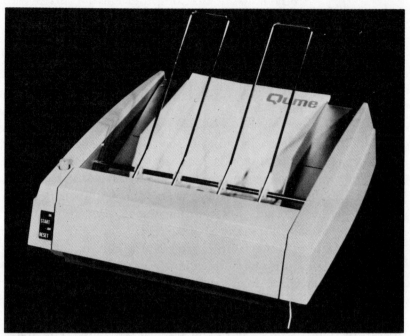

The Qume printer is an example of an impact printer that uses a printing mechanism called a daisy wheel. (*Courtesy Qume Corporation*)

is Diablo) that manufactures a printer using a print element called a daisy wheel. This is a circular print mechanism that spins at a high speed while moving across the paper. The characters are on the ends of petals, which are impacted against a ribbon, thus creating letters on the paper.

Daisy wheel printers are slower than other impact printers (about 45 characters per second), but they create an elegant type of solid character that compares favorably to IBM Selectric type. Also, a daisy wheel printer is much more durable when interfaced to a computer than an electric typewriter.

The disadvantage of daisy wheel printers is their price, which typically begins at about $3000.

Mass Storage Devices

As we mentioned previously, there are two kinds of computer memory. One kind is internal memory, which is memory stored on RAM or ROM integrated circuit chips inside the computer. On a single-board computer, these chips are on the same circuit card as the CPU and I/O circuitry, while in a bus computer, such as the Altair or Heath bus, internal memory chips are on a separate circuit card.

The other kind of computer memory is external memory, which is stored in any one of a number of computer peripherals. In a Radio Shack TRS-80, this peripheral is a cassette recorder. In a Heath H8 computer, you have the option of cassette recorder, paper tape reader, or floppy disk drive. The Altair computer offers you an additional option called a hard disk drive. Digital Systems Corporation offers a digital tape drive for its computer systems, while IBM uses magnetic cartridge tapes in its desktop computer, the IBM 5100 (the closest product IBM has to a personal computer, which starts at about $18,000).

External memory storage is absolutely vital if you wish to have any kind of powerful computer system. The only option is to enter programs line by line into the computer through a keyboard. Some programs consist of several hundred lines, so this process quickly becomes tiresome and impractical. The points of difference between the various kinds of mass storage devices include price, speed, storage capacity, ease of data recovery, and reliability.

The most common mass storage peripheral interfaced to personal computers is the cassette tape recorder. It is cheap, easy to interface to, reliable, and familiar. However, compared to other devices, it is slow (some programs can take up to five minutes to load) and its memory is stored sequentially, making access to information inconvenient and time consuming.

Paper tape readers are generally faster than cassette recorders, but the paper tape itself is awkward to work with and usually can't be read into the computer more than 25 times before another copy has to be generated. Paper tape, which is usually oiled paper, is inexpensive, and you'll need a lot of it. It takes approximately 2000 feet of paper tape to record the same amount of information that can fit on a single 90-minute cassette. If you don't have a Teletype machine to make paper tape copies, then you need a paper tape punch to go along with your paper tape reader which can be quite expensive.

Digital recorders and magnetic cartridge recorders are much faster than cassette tape, store more information per tape, and they are computer-controlled. They have the ability to be "searched" by the computer at high speeds to locate various programs or sections of memory on a tape fairly quickly. Still, their access time can be as long as 40 seconds, which is a considerable improvement over cassette tape recorders but is still not "instantaneous," as is access time with a disk system.

By far the best mass storage unit for use with a personal computer is a disk system. Most of these systems use floppy disks that are made from 0.003-inch mylar covered with a thin layer of magnetic oxides. There are two sizes of floppy disks: regular ones, which are 8 inches in diameter; and "mini floppies," which are 5¼ inches in diameter. Another kind of disk

Pictured here is the Helios disk controller (the two circuit boards are on the left), the Helios disk drive, and a floppy disk. (*Courtesy Processor Technology, Inc.*)

system uses a hard or rigid disk. These systems store a great deal more information than floppy disk units, but they are prohibitively expensive for most personal computer users.

When buying a disk system, you need to concern yourself with its four main components: the disk drive; the disk controller; the floppy disk itself; and the disk system software. Also, you need to be certain that the disk system you are buying is compatible with your computer. There are several disk systems available for the Altair (S-100) bus. Heath offers a mini floppy system for its H8 computer, and at the time of this writing, disk systems are being developed for the TRS-80, Apple, and PET computers.

Information is stored on standard floppy disks on 77 *concentric* circles or tracks. This differs from records that store information on one continuous spiraling track. Even though tracks on the outside of the disk are obviously longer than tracks on the inside of the disk, each track stores the same amount of information. This makes it easier to locate information on a disk even though it isn't the most efficient method of storing data. In addition to tracks, disks are further divided into 26 sectors, which makes it even easier and faster to locate data.

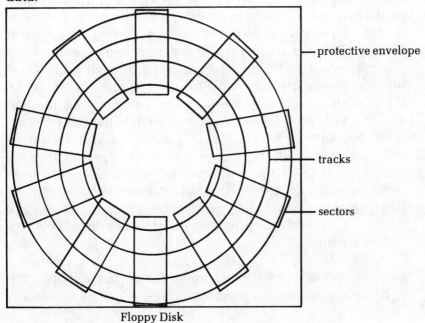

protective envelope

tracks

sectors

Floppy Disk

This format of 77 tracks and 26 sectors is called "IBM standard format." Not all disk systems, including the Altair disk system, use this format. Thus, it is not always possible to write a disk for one system and use it in another. The sectors on a disk are marked with actual holes punched into the disk or with information recorded on the disk. These two methods are called hard sectoring and soft sectoring.

The floppy disk drive is the actual box that is interfaced to a computer. In addition to a slot for inserting floppy disks, a disk drive includes a drive motor that rotates the disk at a high speed and a read/write head controlled by a stepping motor and drive electronics.

The disk controller is a separate circuit card that usually plugs inside the computer (on a Radio Shack computer, the controller will plug into the expansion box). The controller translates program commands from the computer into instructions that the disk drive can understand. Some controllers, like the PerSci 1070, contain their own CPU, while others rely on the CPU already inside the computer.

The most important part of a disk system is its software. Without it, all the fancy hardware in the world isn't worth a nickle. What disk software does is keep track of what is stored on the disk and where. Also, it allows you access to programs by file names or numbers rather than by sector and track number. To store a program on a disk system, you typically enter the word *SAVE* into the computer through a keyboard followed by an arbitrary name for the program. For example, if you wish to store a recipe program, you might instruct the disk to SAVE RECIPE, then when you want to use this program again you can simply enter LOAD RECIPE and the program will almost instantly be loaded into the computer's internal memory. It is this kind of convenience and speed that makes disk systems so desirable. Also, disk systems allow you to run large programs that might be too big for your computer's memory by running the programs a section at a time. This procedure is called *overlays*.

The software for a disk system is called Disk Operating Software or DOS. A good disk operating system will also contain routines for moving programs from one device to another, and it will contain a programming language (usually BASIC) that will communicate with the disk. The programming languages found on the current version of the Radio Shack computer, for example, will not work with a disk system. When Radio Shack comes out with its floppy disk, it will also have to make available a Disk BASIC.

Heath H17, Altair Floppy, and Altair Hard Disk Systems

As with line printers, there are many floppy and hard disk systems available for personal computers. What follows is a review of three of these systems, selected to give you an idea of the differences.

The Heath H17, designed for use with a Heath H8 computer, is a mini floppy disk system costing about $700. It is supplied with a single mini floppy drive that uses a standard 5.25 inch mini disk. It can be expanded to a dual-drive system simply by mounting a second drive into the disk drive chassis.

The storage media is a hard-sectored, 40-track mini floppy disk. The format is 10 sectors per track and 256 bytes per sector, giving it a total storage capacity of 102,000 bytes (102K). Included is a disk operating system that includes disk BASIC and requires 15K bytes of memory. This means that your H8 has to have at least 16K of memory just to operate with a disk system on a minimal basis. Actually, you will need 24K bytes.

To illustrate the speed of this system, the disk BASIC can be loaded into the computer's memory in less than a second. With audio cassette, this procedure would take more than a minute. Heath offers this system in both kit and assembled form. As a kit, you will save approximately $100 from the assembled price of $700.

The Altair Floppy Disk, which is designed for use with an Altair or S-100 compatible computer, is a full-sized disk that uses 8-inch disks capable of storing 310,000 bytes of information (310K). Its disk BASIC requires a minimum of 20K of memory, and it is probably the most powerful software available for a personal computer. The disk itself is hard sectored and does not use IBM standard format.

The controller for the Altair disk consists of two circuit

The Altair Disk Drive (*Courtesy Pertec Computer Corporation*)

boards that plug into the Altair bus. One advanced feature of this system is that it can be interfaced to up to 16 disk drives. This means you could have external memory of 4,960,000 bytes! Cost is approximately $1500.

Before you attach 16 floppy disk drives to your Altair, however, you should be aware of the Altair Hard Disk System, which has a storage capacity of 10,000,000 bytes on a single disk. This system is quite expensive for most personal computer users but is really powerful for many business applications. While there are many different kinds of mini floppy and floppy disk systems available for personal computers, the Altair Hard Disk is the only available hard disk system that I am aware of at this time.

Speechlab

The Speechlab word recognition system that we referred to in chapter 2 consists of an S-100 compatible circuit board connected to a microphone, some software, and a laboratory manual containing 35 experiments you can do with the system. It can be taught to recognize 16 to 64 words (depending upon word size) and to respond differently to each.

The Speechlab has been interfaced successfully to the Sol and Altair computers, and according to the manufacturer, Heuristics, it can be interfaced to any of the S-100 computers.

Software includes a SpeechBASIC programming language that will let you program your computer verbally instead of using keyboard input. The rest of the software includes the necessary programs for controlling the system and a hardware self-test program.

One problem people have detected with Speechlab is its tendency to get confused by background noise, but this can be partially solved by using key words such as *enter* to begin phrases to trigger speech recognition. Also, the system can be taught to verify a phrase by printing it out on a CRT terminal and to correct entries by erasing them. Cost of the Speechlab System at the time of this writing was $299.

Mike

Mike is another speech recognition system that can be interfaced to your personal computer. It has one clear advantage over the Speechlab system in that it can also operate as a

Mike is a speech recognition system that can be connected to a personal computer or operate as a stand-alone unit. (*Courtesy Cartigram Corporation*)

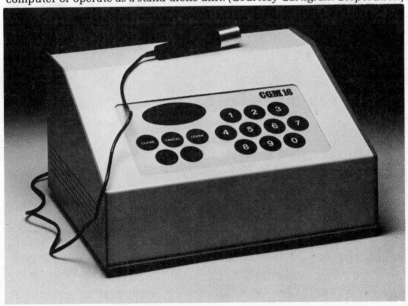

stand-alone system. It doesn't have to be connected to a computer. Manufactured by Centigram Corporation of Sunnyvale, California, Mike is capable of recognizing up to 16 words. Typical vocabularies would include the digits *zero* through *nine* plus the words *enter* and *cancel;* or such words as *left, right, up, down, in, out, start,* and *stop.*

According to company literature, Mike is not intended to replace keyboard input, whether on a computer or a cash register, but rather to augment it to allow an operator whose hands are busy or who finds it impractical or hazardous to operate a keyboard to control equipment with his or her voice. Except when it is in LEARN mode, Mike listens continuously, comparing what it hears to its learned vocabulary in an attempt to recognize words. When a word is recognized, a number representing this word's position in memory appears on Mike's display and a code is sent out of the machine as a control signal.

Music Synthesizer Board

Designed and programmed by Malcolm Wright, the Music Synthesizer Board from Solid State Music is another example of the many fine plug-in circuit cards available for Altair (S-100) bus computers. Today, there are over 300 circuit cards on the market that plug into this bus.

To use this device, you first plug it into the computer and then connect it through a two-pin plug on the card to a stereo amplifier or PA amplifier. Next, you enter the software that controls this board into the computer line by line through your keyboard. You only need do this once, because you can store the program on cassette tape, paper tape, or on a floppy disk. Once you accomplish this, you are ready to play music. The synthesizer board and software uses standard ASCII notation for music encoding, making it easy to write and correct musical tunes. To play a C note, you enter C on your keyboard. For sharp or flat notes, you enter a " + " or a " − " sign.

The board will simulate the sounds of a harpsichord, cello, organ, or flute. It isn't really capable of simulating a trumpet, violin, piano, or bass drum, but you can still play some pretty impressive music including Bach, Handel's *Messiah*, and the Beatles' *Norwegian Wood*, to name a few. To play music that is really impressive, you need at least two of these boards so one note can play off of another. The software will control up to five cards at a time (making for a quintet).

When this board was first introduced, it sold for $250. Now that the engineering and design costs have been covered, its price has dropped significantly. The last price I was aware of was $149.95. As personal computers become more popular, price reductions such as this can be expected.

The TV Dazzler

Manufactured by Cromemco, the TV Dazzler is two circuit cards designed to fit into an S-100 or Altair-type computer. It lets you interface your computer to a standard color television set for color graphics, color alphanumeric display, or color animation.

Combined with an optional "joystick" that includes four push-button switches (to program however you like) and a built-in audio speaker, the TV Dazzler can be used to play some spectacular computer games including the popular game Life. Without the joystick, you can still play many keyboard-controlled games and you can use the Dazzler to draw beautiful charts and graphs.

Summary

One of the biggest fears computer marketers have is that their customers will discover they have far more computing power than they really need. Many people buying $20,000 computer systems could get by quite nicely with $10,000 systems, and many people buying $10,000 systems could do the same application with $5000 systems. This buyer's guide to computer hardware was written to give you a taste of the potential power of personal computing. It should serve as a basis for further exploration of computer products. Believe

The number of plug-in compatible circuits for S-100 computers is nearly endless. Pictured here is a 16K RAM memory board from Digital Micro Systems. (*Courtesy Digital Micro Systems*)

me, the range of personal computers, minicomputers, video terminals, line printers, disk storage systems, plug-in compatible circuit cards, is endless. Careful shopping in this field can save you a lot of money and hassle. Whether your budget for a computer is $500 or $50,000, you can always find a way to get more computer power for the money. Start with a general idea of what you want to do with a computer. Make some basic decisions as to what kind of system will do the job. If you need a line printer with good quality type, you'll probably prefer a daisy wheel printer over a matrix printer. If you want to store a lot of information and have instant access to it, you won't be able to get by with a cassette recorder or a paper tape reader; you'll need a disk system. The next question is: Do you need a hard disk, a floppy disk, or a mini floppy disk? If you want to do text editing with your computer, you may need a keyboard with upper- and lower-case letters and a line printer with upper- and lower-case letters. If you want to use the computer for home budgeting, playing games, and running educational programs, an inexpensive complete system such as the PET or Radio Shack may provide you with all the computing power you need. Take your time and use your head; a good computer system could change your life.

8

THE PERSONAL COMPUTING SCENE

ALL WATCHED OVER BY MACHINES OF LOVING GRACE
by Richard Brautigan

I like to think (and
the sooner the better!)
of a cybernetic meadow
where mammals and computers
live together in mutually
programming harmony
like pure water
touching clear sky.

I like to think
(right now, please!)
of a cybernetic forest
filled with pines and electronics
where deer stroll peacefully
past computers
as if they were flowers
with spinning blossoms.

I like to think
  (it has to be!)
of a cybernetic ecology
where we are free of our labors
and joined back to nature,
returned to our mammal
brothers and sisters,
and all watched over
by machines of loving grace.*

Before the Altair

While the introduction of the Altair computer in January 1975 is considered the beginning point of personal computers, there were people involved in personal computing before then. These were people who worked for computer companies, private industry, or schools who realized computers had the potential to do great things for society and for the individual. They had access to computers and used them for purposes other than what management thought they should be doing.

In the late 1960s these underground personal computing enthusiasts became known as computer freaks. The people they worked for generally tolerated their activities because then, as now, it was hard to find qualified people to program and run computers. By and large, these computer freaks were typical radicals in their early or late twenties who realized the power of computers and foresaw the day when everyone would have one. They did practically anything, including working for little or no pay, just to be close to a computer. Many of the games and educational programs used on today's personal computers were first developed by computer freaks.

One of these early pioneers was Bob Albrecht, who likes to sign his name as The Dragon. Bob started a nonprofit organization in the San Francisco Bay area called People's Com-

*Excerpted from *The Pill Versus the Springhill Mine Disaster* by Richard Brautigan. Copyright © 1968 by Richard Brautigan. Reprinted by permission of Delacorte Press/Seymour Lawrence.

puter Company. This group sponsored seminars, published newsletters and books, wrote software, and generally advocated computer power long before the days of handheld calculators. Today, Bob Albrecht is one of the leading advocates of personal computers in education. His book, *My Computer Likes Me When I Speak BASIC*, has outsold all other BASIC language textbooks, and he is the guiding force at Dymax Publications, which publishes a monthly magazine called *Calculator/Computer* and several personal computing books.

People like Bob Albrecht and the People's Computer Company are important because they laid the groundwork for many of today's personal computing activities. As this chapter shows, it was important groundwork that led not only to popular acceptance of the computer itself but also to an entire cult. Today computer hobbyists are everywhere.

Hobby Clubs

Today there are several hundred computer hobby clubs ranging from highly structured groups of 10,000 members to clubs of four or five people. One enterprising hobbyist, Ernie Brooner, started a one-man computer club in Lakeside, Montana. Soon he found that his club was listed in several magazines and he began receiving newsletters, promotional literature, and personal letters from across the country. According to Brooner, the main advantage of his club was that no one could outvote him; and the main disadvantage was that there was no one to talk to, to learn from, or share experiences with.

While computer hobby clubs were inevitable, the original clubs were organized directly as a result of a marketing strategy initiated by Ed Roberts and Mits. Because the Altair was a mail-order product that you had to buy directly from the factory, there was no way you could see one unless you were lucky enough to have a friend who took the plunge before you did. With all the publicity that the Altair received, this situation was less than ideal; and it became important for Mits to develop a quick method for demonstrating the Altair throughout the country.

The idea that Roberts came up with was to equip a camper van called the Mitsmobile with an Altair computer system and drive it through the country stopping at shopping centers, hotels, schools—any place where people could come aboard and try out the new personal computer. This concept quickly grew to the point where Mits was renting convention space in motels and presenting four-hour seminars followed by hands-on demonstrations of equipment. The van became a mere transportation vehicle for the Altair system and the seminar instructors. Hundreds of people attended these meetings from coast to coast and in many cases stayed after the presentation to form informal study groups that grew into computer clubs. The Southern California Computer Society, which is now called the International Computer Society, began in this fashion. Today, with over 10,000 members, it is the largest computer club in the world.

Most of the original computer clubs tend to be highly technical groups of engineers and programmers deeply involved in personal computing. Their meetings are often highlighted by the presentation of technical papers or by debates over the intricacies of various esoteric aspects of computer hardware. The reason for this is simply because the Altair and most personal computing products that followed it required a certain amount of electronic know-how just to build them. The literature that came with these products was crude, and quite often you could not get a personal computer in operation without doing some of your own troubleshooting.

Today, many computer clubs have broadened their appeal to attract novices in the personal computing scene, and indeed many newcomers have formed their own clubs. The Ventura County Computer Society, headquartered in Oxnard, California, has formed a subgroup of its members interested in business applications and commercial activities with personal computers. If you live in the San Diego area, you can join any one of four subgroups of the San Diego Computer Society including: hardware, systems support, software, and applications. The Chicago Computer Club, CACHE, offers a clinic on the basics of programming and has sponsored some very interesting presentations by personal computer manufacturers.

The activities of computer clubs vary greatly from one club to another. Some clubs, like the Sol Users' Society (SOLUS), are formed for people who have the same computer system. These clubs exchange computer programs, information on hardware, and so forth, and they try to influence the direction of the manufacturer (in this case, Processor Technology) by reporting on their experiences and suggesting product improvements. Other clubs, like the Rhode Island Computer Hobbyists (RICH), are formed to disseminate general information to all interested parties. RICH, for example, has sponsored presentations on solar energy projects, terminals for the deaf, and reviews of products like the Heathkit computer.

Clubs oftentimes sponsor special personal computing events. The Louisville Area Computer Club, for instance, is holding the first Micro-Chess tourney and plans to make it an annual event. The Computer Network of Kansas City has been looking into the possibility of making an education program for the local public television station while the Southern California Computer Society has sponsored seminars on computer music and computer art, the latter having been held at the Academy of Motion Picture Arts and Sciences in Los Angeles.

Two activities that seem to be common among most clubs are publishing a club newsletter and sponsoring the group purchase of computer products. Club newsletters vary from slick magazines, such as the one put out by the International Computer Society (formerly SCCS), to the publication of single-page mimeographed sheets. The idea of group purchase (several members get together to buy the same product and thus receive a quantity discount) is basically sound and can save club members a lot of cash. However, there have been cases where clubs have lost money when manufacturers were unable to deliver products as promised.

The main advantage of a club is that it can become a source of help and advice to both beginning and experienced personal computer users. As the market continues to grow, clubs that are less interested in the technical nuances of computer hardware and more interested in how you can use a computer will undoubtedly spring up across the country. A list of some of today's major computer clubs is provided in Appendix C. If there isn't a club in your area, you might ask someone at the nearest computer store or you can look in computer hobbyist magazines (see pages 142–147) for club information. *Byte* magazine carries a regular column called "Clubs and Newsletters," which keeps up on the activity of computer clubs and announces the formation of new groups.

Personal Computing Shows

By November 1975, just 11 months after the announcement of the Altair computer, Mits was facing very serious growth problems. For one thing, the building they were housed in was woefully inadequate. The advertising and technical publication agency was located away from the main administrative and manufacturing office, and the software department was even farther away, located around the far corner. People were wasting time just walking back and forth between the various divisions of the company, to say nothing of other more serious problems.

Mainly because of the huge backlog of orders, Mits wasn't able to support the Altair as fast as Roberts had promised. Many products were months behind, and production schedules seemed to be slipping daily. The repair department was hopelessly clogged with a poorly designed 4K memory board. This situation helped to create a void in the market that was soon being filled by other companies. One of these companies was Processor Technology, which was started by a young engineer named Bob Marsh who literally began his company by peddling memory boards to members of the Homebrew Computer Club in San Francisco.

Roberts and I were in his office discussing this situation, looking for a PR way to help us rebuild the confidence of our customers. He said, "We need to do something exciting." As small as we were at the time (about 60 employees), we were running full-page advertisements in *Scientific American,* *Popular Electronics, Radio Electronics,* and a number of technical publications. These ads were costing us $20,000 a month and they were bringing in more and more orders to add to our backlog. We were going big time fast and we needed a way to prove to our customers that we could keep up with the times. Many of them had been patient with us for too long. While Altair, besides being a product, was something *you believed in*, we were holding people's money for products like the Altair Floppy Disk, which hadn't even been prototyped yet.

I suggested to Roberts that once we moved into a new building we hold a national convention. I had gotten this idea from attending the National Computer Conference in Anaheim earlier that spring. It seemed to me that personal computing was something quite different from the regular computer market and therefore needed its own convention. It needed to reach a different audience than the people inside the computer industry. It needed to go beyond that to the public.

Roberts said, "It's a crazy idea, but it's your neck, so go ahead with it." Although Roberts, who was a very impatient man to begin with, was eager to hold the conference as soon as possible, I managed to persuade him to hold off and schedule the event for March 1976. In the interim we would have plenty of time to move into our new building near the Albuquerque airport and prepare for the convention.

We called the convention the World Altair Computer Convention, or WACC, and went ahead promoting it through our mailing lists, through our users' group publication, *Computer Notes*, and through press releases and magazine advertisements. The day before the WACC, Ed Roberts called in the key Mits people to his office and said he felt like it was the day before D-Day. The WACC would either make us or break us. We had invited the editors of *Popular Electronics*, *Radio Electronics*, *Byte*, *Interface Age* and the president of the Southern California Computer Society and others to be speakers at this convention. The SCCS had chartered a special airplane for the flight to Albuquerque. Our two new competitors, Processor Technology and Cromemco, would be there to present their equipment. The attention of computer hobbyists would be on Mits to see if the company had eliminated its production problems and could now live up to its promises. They would take a tour through the manufacturing plant so that we could show them that we really had the capability to meet their needs and that we were an honest bunch of people.

As show promoter, my biggest fear was that no one would show up. By this time, we had spent about $20,000 on the promotion and production of this show and we had promised to give away some $4,000 worth of door prizes including one of our new floppy disk units. That evening I went up to the nearby Albuquerque Marina Hotel to see if there was any activity. The parking lot was crowded and people—from Colorado, Texas, California, Arizona, and many faraway places—were getting out of their cars, unloading luggage. We had reserved the entire hotel, about 200 rooms, so I knew these people were here for the convention. The publicity had worked; we wouldn't have to pay for the empty rooms we reserved, and more important, I was still employed.

The next morning there were long lines of people winding down the corridors of the hotel. People were waiting to register for the convention before we could even open up the registration tables. I went into a panic, afraid that we would probably blow the whole event, handling it so badly that nobody would ever buy an Altair again. It would be the end of a dream.

Luckily for me and for Mits, the Marketing Manager was a very well-organized woman named Pam Holloman who saw to it that the ticket tables were set up correctly and that all the events of this two-day affair ran smoothly. Pam went on to become a vice-president at Mits and today she is a very successful personal computer marketer for Pertec Computer Corporation and one of the leading women in the business.

The program at the WACC, which became the first of a series of personal computing conventions, consisted of an opening presentation by Ed Roberts, seminars on various hardware and software aspects of Altair products by Mits engineers and programmers, an exhibit of Altair systems and add-on products made by Processor Technology and Cromemco, an exhibit of hobbyist computer systems including a computerized backgammon game, a computer-controlled ham radio station, and a computer chess game, plus a marathon speakers' presentation that evening followed by more exhibits and an awards banquet the following day.

The hit speaker at the WACC was Ted Nelson, author of *Computer Lib* and more recently, *The Home Computer Revolution*. As a visionary, Ted was one of the first to see the real implications of this new technology. His ideas for implementing personal computers and his ability to predict what is going to happen in this market have proven to be amazingly accurate. Ted predicted at the WACC that the computer hobbyist market would level off at 100,000 or so and be replaced by a much bigger consumer market; that computers would recapitulate the history of high fidelity and become as common as Garrard turntables; and that the computer industry would be liberated by computer hobbyists.*

Ted proved to be right about many of his predictions and attitudes, and today he is a leading figure in the personal computing industry as well as the main speaker at many personal computing conventions and banquets.

Other speakers at the first personal computer gathering were Les Solomon, the editor at *Popular Electronics* who had stuck his neck out to put the Altair on the cover of his January issue; Larry Steckler, the editor of *Radio Electronics;* Carl Helmers, the editor and creator of *Byte* magazine; David Ahl, publisher of *Creative Computing;* Lou Fields, vice-president and later president of the Southern California Computer Society; and Ward Spaniol, the current president of SCCS.

The last event at the WACC was the awards banquet where we awarded prizes to the computer hobbyists who had brought their Altair systems and demonstrated them. Don Alexander of Columbus, Ohio, was the grand prize winner of an Altair Floppy Disk for his demonstration of a computer controlled amateur radio Teletype station. Tied for second place was Randy Miller of Tempe, Arizona, who demonstrated a chess-playing computer program on an Altair with 20K of memory; and Wirt and Valerie Atmar of Las Cruces, New Mex-

*From *Computer Notes,* April 1976.

ico, who demonstrated a speech synthesizer that was computer controlled by the Altair. This was March 1976, a year and a half before the Radio Shack computer was announced. These people were true computer pioneers, doing things with Altairs that they built themselves that at the time of this writing still haven't become standard applications.

Needless to say, the WACC was a very successful event for Mits. Subsequent magazine articles on the WACC were numerous and positive and the 700 or so people who came from every state in the union and 11 foreign countries went home with good impressions of the company. Production and morale greatly improved and Mits went on to dominate the

Personal computer shows are a good place to learn about computers and see all the latest equipment.

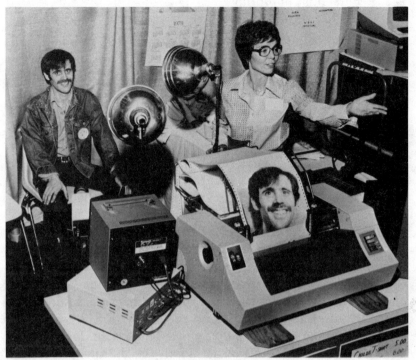

Part of the fun in attending a personal computer show is having your picture taken by—guess what?—a computer.

personal computing industry for more than a year before much larger firms got into the game.

John Dilkes, an amateur radio enthusiast and computer hobbyist, decided to promote a national personal computing show in Atlantic City in August 1976. By this time, there were more than 50 companies in the personal computing industry and they were hungry for a show sponsored by an independent group. Using the same basic format as the WACC, Dilkes was able to draw a crowd of over 3000 and approximately 40 exhibitors, and the personal computer show was born. Today there are annual personal computing expositions in New York, Chicago, Los Angeles, San Francisco, Detroit, Boston, Philadelphia, London, and Montreal, and many other cities. They are probably the best places to get acquainted with the many aspects of personal computing in a relatively short time.

One of the most successful computer shows was the Personal Computer Show held in Chicago in October 1977. Over

12,000 people paid $10 each to see close to 100 personal computing exhibits; many staying for one or more of the many seminars and special presentations. Gene Murrow, president of Computer Power and Light of Studio City, California, conducted a special personal computing school with classes in BASIC language programming and small business applications. By attending this class, you learned while sitting at the terminal of one of Gene's fine Compal computers. Other programs at this convention included: Turning Your Computer Hobby Into a Computer Career, presented by Digital Equipment Corporation; Math Packages for Business Computers, presented by Gerald Koppel of the AAA Chicago Computer Center; The Appliance of Tomorrow, Today, by Dan Merkling of Home Computer Services in Salt Lake; Introduction to Hardware by E & L Instruments; Impact of Home Computers on Ham Radio by Bryan Leipper of the American Radio Relay League; Introduction to Microprocessors and a series of related technical seminars by Sybex; The Office Communication Center by Micro Plaza; What the Future Holds for Robotics by the United States Robotic Society; and many others.

As personal computing shows develop, they seem to get better and better. Usually these events last three or four days, and they are excellent places to see all the latest personal computing equipment, hear from the experts, get your questions answered, learn what personal computing is all about, find out how to use a personal computer, and even solve your own particular computing problems. To find out about personal computing shows, you need to subscribe to one or more of the personal computing magazines, which we will examine next.

Personal Computing Magazines

The first personal computing publication was *Computer Notes,* a Mits tabloid that went out to all the Altair users and was also distributed through Mits retail stores and to computer hobby clubs. *Computer Notes* was considerably different from the technical newsletters of the established computer companies in that it concentrated on the human aspects of computing. In addition to information useful to Altair owners, it kept track of what people were using their Altairs for, and it promoted the entrepreneurial instincts of many original Altair owners.

Today there are a number of major national personal computing magazines, each of them emphasizing different aspects of the market and the people using computers. The ones that should be of most interest to you are described here.

BYTE MAGAZINE

Byte was the first computer hobbyist magazine. There are many conflicting stories about who actually started the publication and this conflict still divides much of the industry. Many believe that the person responsible was Wayne Green, publisher of a ham magazine called *73,* who was listed as publisher on the first issue; but some feel that the credit belonged to Green's former wife, Virginia Peshke. Today, Virginia is the publisher of *Byte,* which has grown to be the leading personal computing magazine with a circulation of over 100,000, while Wayne Green is the publisher of *Kilobaud,* a competitive magazine.

The editorial content of *Byte* was conceived of and is today controlled by Editor-in-Chief Carl Helmers. *Byte* was the first publication to see the commercial growth, to say nothing of the potential advertising revenue, of personal computers. It has done a good job serving the hobbyist aspects of computing with many advanced technical articles and do-it-yourself projects. It is the "meat and potatoes" technical journal of the personal computing industry. However, for beginners in personal computing, and for those interested only in how to use computers, not how they work internally, *Byte* is really far too advanced and technical.

Byte is published monthly by Byte Publications, Inc., 70 Main St., Peterborough, NH 03458. Subscriptions are $15 for one year, $27 for two years, and $39 for three years in the United States and its possessions. In Canada and Mexico the cost is $17.50 for one year, $32 for two years, and $46.50 for three years.

INTERFACE AGE MAGAZINE

Like *Byte* magazine, *Interface Age* was embroiled in controversy during its early days. It began as the official publication of the Southern California Computer Society, but a dispute between SCCS and *Interface Age* led Jones to split the magazine off into an independent publication.

While *Interface Age* is somewhat technical, its editorial content is quite a bit different from *Byte*. It is basically an application-oriented magazine that features many programs and software information. A true indication of this fact is that it periodically publishes a plastic record insert called the Floppy ROM that contains computer programs. All you have to do is play the record, record it on cassette tape, and feed it into your computer. *Interface Age* also publishes a periodic hardware issue featuring press releases from most personal computer manufacturers. These releases are nicely arranged into categories such as systems, line printers, video displays, mainframes, etc.

A subscription to *Interface Age* (published monthly) is $14 a year in the United States, $16 in Canada and Mexico. To subscribe, send a check to *Interface Age* Magazine, PO Box 1234, Seritos, CA 90701.

KILOBAUD

Published by Wayne Green, *Kilobaud* is a computer hobbyist magazine that is considerably less technical than *Byte,* aimed more at beginning hobbyists and at small business users. *Kilobaud* is one of the more useful publications in terms of things you can do with your computer. It has a small business computing section and carries many interesting programs you can run in your computer to play games or perform household functions. Billed as the magazine that's "understandable for beginners; interesting for experts," *Kilobaud* lives up to most of its promises. It is a very good publication.

Kilobaud is published monthly by 1001001, Inc., Peterborough, NH 03458. Subscriptions in the United States and Canada are $15 for one year and $36 for three years.

CALCULATORS/COMPUTERS

This magazine advertises itself as being for home and school computing, though it would seem to be mostly for school computing. It contains many fundamental articles that teach you about calculators and computers and how to use them. Included are self-contained instructional units which can be reproduced for classroom use. These units are designed for students at primary, secondary, and college levels. *Calculators/Computers* contains a lot of interesting programs and fun exercises like puzzles and games. Bob Albrecht, the "Dragon" who started People's Computer Company, is the guiding force.

A subscription to *Calculators/Computers* is $12 a year for seven issues, $17 a year surface mail for Canada, $23 airmail to Canada, $28 airmail to Europe and Pan America. Published by Dymax, PO Box 310, Menlo Park, CA 94025.

CREATIVE COMPUTING

This magazine came out of the computer "freak" movement and is today complete with R. Crumb's cartoons reproduced in brilliant color and a lot of juvenile design aimed at college and high school students. Many of its articles appear to be papers written for graduate school degrees. It covers a broad range of personal computing subjects and tries to concentrate on applications and software. Published bimonthly by Creative Computing, Box 789-M, Morristown, NJ 07960. Subscriptions are $8 for one year, $15 for two years, and $21 for three years.

PEOPLE'S COMPUTERS

Published by People's Computer Company, *People's Computers* recently started SPOT, the Society of PET Owners and Trainers for people who own PET computers. SPOT is a forum for people to swap software, ideas, and experiences. It is typical of the novel and useful services provided by this magazine.

People's Computers carries a broad range of articles aimed at students and teachers. The staff is not afraid to criticize manufacturers for foul-ups nor to predict the social impact of personal computers on our society.

Subscriptions are $8 a year for six issues, $15 for two

years. Send your check to: People's Computer Company, 1263 El Camino Real, Box E, Menlo Park, CA 94025.

PERSONAL COMPUTING

By the fall of 1976 it was apparent to me that the hobby market was rapidly nearing its peak. The personal computer market was going to be a consumer, small business market. The future belonged to ordinary people: housewives, professionals, laborers, teachers, doctors, mechanics, retailers, and even janitors. I felt that *Byte, Kilobaud,* and *Interface Age* weren't really serving this new group of personal computer users, so I left Mits to start a publication for Benwill Publishing of Boston that would try to bridge the gap between the technical people and the public. This publication was *Personal Computing,* which I published for a year before deciding to move on to other things. At the time of this writing, it remains the only truly consumer-oriented magazine of any significance (a promising competitor, *ROM,* has never seemed to get off the ground).

Personal Computing is graphically designed to look like a good quality newsstand magazine, making it stand out from the hobbyist publications. It has a lot of application articles and is aimed at beginners who don't necessarily want to become hobbyists but would like to be computer users. A large percentage of readers are professional people including accountants, doctors, lawyers, and teachers.

A subscription to *Personal Computing,* a monthly publication, is $14 a year in the United States, $18 in Canada and Mexico. Send a check to: Benwill Publishing, 1050 Commonwealth Ave., Boston, MA 02215.

SBC MAGAZINE

SBC, or *Small Business Computers Magazine,* is for people who want to use computers in their small businesses. It contains articles on how to use computers for inventory systems, order entry systems, general ledgers, payroll, etc. *SBC* tells you how to set systems up for these kinds of applications and review current business systems on the market.

One of the more interesting articles I have seen in this

magazine was one by Don Truesdell entitled "We Needed a Way to Grow" showing how his small firm was able to grow rapidly yet remain a family business with only six employees.* Truesdell set up a computer in his company so that he could handle many more orders and automatically keep track of inventory. If an order is out of stock, the computer automatically puts it on backlog. It can display the customer's record, including dollar sales, payment history, and credit rating. The order can be retained on a disk memory or it can be printed out immediately on a three-part form that contains a picking list, acknowledgement, and packing slip. When the order has been filled and shipped, the computer prints an invoice, reduces the inventory record, and updates the accounts receivable record. The goal of Truesdell's company has been to increase its yearly business from $1 million to $5 million without having to increase the size of the company or the number of employees.

Published monthly by *SBC Magazine*, Box 305, Dover, NY 07801; subscriptions are $12 per year.

OTHER MAGAZINES

Many magazines today are carrying information about personal computers and how to use them. Included are *Popular Electronics*, *Radio Electronics*, *Scientific American*, *Popular Science*, and *Modern Electronics*. Also, most of the computer clubs have their own publications, which range from nice, glossy magazines to single-page mimeographed sheets. There are computer retailing publications like *Computer Retailing* (W. R. C. Smith Publishing, 1760 Peachtree Rd. NW, Atlanta, GA 30357) and *Computer Dealer* (Gordon Publications, Inc., 20 Community Place, Morristown, NJ 07960); and there are industry newsletters including *Subroutines* (208 Dartmouth NE, Albuquerque, NM 87106), published by myself, and the *Kilobaud Newsletter* (Peterborough, NH 03458), published by Wayne Green. Information on these can be obtained by writing to the addresses given.

---

*"We Needed a Way to Grow," *SBC Magazine*, November/December 1977.

Computer Stores

The main problem with computers was always how to market them. People who bought personal computers through the mail from Mits and from some of its imitators found that it was hard to get answers to their many questions. The letters they wrote (by the thousands) and the many phone calls only added to the difficulty. Everyone at Mits in the marketing and engineering department spent most of their daytime working hours trying to deal with these inquisitive and sometimes irate customers. The only real work at Mits had to be done at night.

In the summer of 1975 this all began to change when Dick and Lois Heiser opened up the world's first computer retail store in Los Angeles. By the end of the year, a couple dozen stores were opened in the United States and by the end of 1976, at least 100 computer retail stores were operating. Today the number has climbed over 1000 according to some estimates. (See Appendix A for a selected list of over 500 of these.)

The most important aspect of a computer store then and now is that it is a place to go to get first-hand information. The people who run these new frontier establishments are usually quite familiar with the computers they sell. They are in the front lines of the computer retailing effort and have to deal with the many problems people have in setting up computer systems. As one retailer put it, "My suppliers work in nice, safe factories, but that's plate glass on the front of my store. I'm vulnerable when the customers are mad.*

There are many arguments among marketers about the ability of computer stores to remain viable, prosperous businesses in the face of competition from department stores and from electronics stores such as Radio Shack. Some say that retail stores will not be able to keep up with the advertising, distribution, and customer-relations strength of these more experienced competitors. Yet a computer system is not as simple to sell as a washing machine or even a stereo system. It is hard

*Nels Winkless III, "A Look at Computer Retailing." *Personal Computing*, March/April 1977, p. 93.

to imagine the Sears appliance man explaining to someone the differences between a mini floppy, floppy, and hard disk drive.

Computers require much more support than most other consumer products. Experiences of computer retailers show that it takes an *average* of three hours selling time with each customer before they buy a computer and five hours afterwards! A good retail store carries several types of computers and all the various accessories and peripherals that make up a computer system. The store has to know how to repair computers, how to program computers, and how to set up various customized systems for special applications. Many stores offer night and weekend classes on the basics of personal computers, and many serve as meeting places for computer clubs. All of them carry a wide selection of books and magazines.

Computer retailers, with their day-to-day experiences with computers and people using computers, have been able to see the many technical gaps in the product lines of their suppliers, and in many cases they have filled these gaps with their own technology. Before Mits could develop a hard disk system, their retail store in Atlanta developed one of their own. Another Altair dealer, tired of waiting for Mits to develop multi-user BASIC, went ahead and wrote this software. Even the customers have gotten into the act, designing their own special circuit cards for the S-100 bus or their own special software application packages. This has helped to give the personal computing industry a "cottage industry" flavor that is bound to continue for many years.

Computer stores will probably become a common part of the American scene and spread to all parts of the world. They will become more professional, better capitalized, and many of the original retailers will undoubtedly sell out and move to other things, thus making room for more sophisticated stores. Already there are several franchises and licensed computer retail store chains including the Byte shops with over 80 stores throughout the United States and Canada.

In an interview I did with Disk Heiser in the fall of 1975 he said, "People in this business haven't been optimistic enough. I've tried to be as optimistic as possible, but that has turned out to be too conservative. You have to be wildly optimistic." As wildly optimistic as Heiser was, I doubt that he realized how fast his concept would catch on.

What the Future Holds

Many people believe that over the next few years home computers will be so successfully mass-marketed that they will compete with television as recreational devices. The interactive computer TV screen with its dazzling graphics and broad array of games and programs will become more fascinating to many people than Archie Bunker and hopefully more useful than Johnny Carson. Already, video games are becoming a factor in the TV rating system. This aspect of home computing alone could have a major impact on people's lives and the way businesses merchandize and operate.

But will personal computers really give us the power to change society? Will they alter the basic social structure, the basic life patterns of our citizens? It is only by doing this that they can truly be revolutionary.

In this book I have tried to give you a glimpse at the potential of this new product and enough information and incentive to get involved. Knowing what you know now, just imagine the significance of personal computers when they can be tied together in mass communication networks, so that personal computer owners can communicate instantly with one another, share programs, ideas, and huge central memory banks of information. Already hobbyists and forward-looking computer companies are busily at work on just such a project. Using a device called a modem, personal computers are communicating to one another over the phone lines. In the future, a national personal computing network will serve as the basis for an electronic mailing system to replace our antiquated postal system. Instead of writing a letter, putting the letter into an envelope, licking a stamp, dropping it in a mail box, you will be able to instantly deliver your message to anyone or most any place in the world. Other advantages of computer networks are the prospects of tying into the banking system so that home owners and businesses can do their banking right at the computer terminal. You will be able to tap into libraries of information that may include consumer information such as the comparison of grocery prices in your area, the ratings of restaurants, or a list of entertainment events. Much of your shopping can be done at the terminal. Just place your order for a new sofa, transfer funds from your bank account to the store's account, and it will be delivered to you the next day. Some people will be able to do much of their work at home because they can bring the office right into their study via computer. Computer networks will allow us to again operate in smaller economic and social units. This possibility of a return to a simpler, less intense life-style is one of the truly revolutionary (and ironic!) aspects of personal computing.

Ed Roberts's original concept of personal computing was to provide everyone with a low-cost computer terminal that could communicate to a central computer over the phone lines. A year before the Altair computer was announced, we were busily laying the groundwork for just such a system. One of our employees was even sent out to compare grocery prices at several stores just so we could begin to understand the process of providing this type of information. An under-$400 computer terminal with a built-in modem (the Compter 256) was designed and manufactured. A complete BASIC programming course and operational manual was prepared. And then along came Altair, and the idea was forgotten. The centralized computer was turned over to the marketing department to handle order entry and inventory. Oftentimes, I have wondered how personal computing might be radically different if we had gone ahead with our computer network instead of developing a stand-alone computer.

One area of our lives that will be changed radically is the manner in which we educate ourselves and our children. By using a personal computer to accumulate the facts and store the information that you need to know about history, mathematics, biology, and other fields, you can free your mind to learn how to manipulate and use this information. In today's schools we waste an inordinate amount of time simply accumulating and memorizing information. With further miniaturization of electronic components it will become possible to design computer systems as small as handheld calculators. These computers will become our personal calculating and memory aids. Who was the president of Bolivia in 1927? Once you've programmed your handheld computer to remember this fact, it will never forget and you needn't agonize over it.

Improvements in speech recognition and further development of artificial intelligence will lead to dramatic advances in the art of robotics. Already the United States Robotics Society is busily sponsoring the development of "pet" robots to entertain and babysit our children, act as security guards, and provide us with companionship. Household robots will soon be manufactured to do our dishes, answer the door and the telephone, mow the lawn, and feed the dog. Dozens of articles in personal computing magazines are already speculating on how this can be done. Hobbyists have built the prototypes of these robots. The implications are endless.

It is impossible, of course, to accurately forecast the development of new technological products. Very few science fiction books depict the use of personal computers, yet we now know they will have a major impact on our future. We know that we are entering a brave new world of technology, that the stakes are high, and that the results will be interesting at the least. Armed with the information I've given you, I hope you will visit a computer store, find out if there is a hobby club in your area, and subscribe to a personal computing magazine. You need to get involved. Everyone does.

APPENDIX A:
COMPUTER STORES

A discussion of computer stores (how they operate, what you should look for) is included on pages 148–150. While there are over 1000 retail stores doing business throughout the United States today including a few chain operations, space limitations demand selectivity. Therefore, the following list has been edited to include the most accessible, active stores around. We extend our apologies to any that have been overlooked.

ALABAMA

Computerland
3020 University Dr. NW
Huntsville AL 35805

The Computer Center
Terry Woodward
303B Poplar Place
Birmingham, AL 35209

ALASKA

Team Electronics
Country Village Shopping
      Center
700 East Benson Blvd.
Anchorage, AK 99503

Team Electronics
404 East Fireweed Lane
Anchorage, AK 99503

Team Electronics
1698 Airport Way
Fairbanks, AK 99701

ARIZONA

Altair Computer Center
4941 East 29th St.
Tucson, AZ 85711

Ancrona Corp.
4518 East Broadway
Tucson, AZ 85711

Arizona Micro Systems
3240 West Larkspur Dr.
Phoenix, AZ 85029

Bits & Bytes Computer Shop
6819-C North 21st Ave.
Phoenix, AZ 85015

Byte Phoenix
813 North Scottsdale Rd.
Tempe, AZ 85281

Byte Shops of Arizona
813 North Scottsdale Rd.
Tempe, AZ 85281

Desert Data Computer Store
P.O. Box 1334
Tucson, AZ 85702

ARKANSAS

Computer Products Unlimited
2412 South Broadway
Little Rock, AR 72204

CALIFORNIA

Action Audio Electronics
285 Lake Merced Blvd.
Daly City, CA 94015

Ancrona Corp.
P.O. Box 2208-P
Culver City, CA 90230

Ancrona Corp.
11080 Jefferson Blvd.
Culver City, CA 90230

Ancrona Corp.
1300-D East Edinger Ave.
Santa Ana, CA 92705

Applied Computer Technology
2465 Fourth St.
Berkeley, CA 94610

A-VID Electronics Co.
1655 East 28th St.
Long Beach, CA 90806

Bargain Electronics Enterprises
2018 Lomita Blvd., No. 1
Lomita, CA 90717

Bits, Bytes & Pieces
6211 Quincewood Circle
Citrus Heights, CA 95710

Bits 'N Bytes
679 D.S. State College Blvd.
Fullerton, CA 92631

Bootstrap Computer Store
24 St. Component Shop
3981 24th St.
San Francisco, CA 94114

Bootstrap Computer Store
3981 24th St.
San Francisco, CA 94114

Byte
18424 Ventura Blvd.
Tarzana, CA 91356

Byte Citrus Heights
6041 Greenback Lane
Citrus Heights, CA 95610

Byte Lawndale
16508 Hawthorne Blvd.
Lawndale, CA 90260

Byte Pasadena
496 South Lake Ave.
Pasadena, CA 91101

Byte San Diego
5375 Kearny Villa Rd.
San Diego, CA 92123

Byte San Mateo
1200 West Hillsdale Blvd.
San Mateo, CA 74403

Byte Santa Barbara
3 West Mission St.
Santa Barbara, CA 93101

Byte Shop
1514 University Ave.
Berkeley, CA 94703

Byte Shop
2559 South Bascom Ave.
Campbell, CA 95008

Byte Shop
1063 West El Camino Real
Mountain View, CA 94040

Byte Shop
321 Pacific Ave.
San Francisco, CA 94111

Byte Shop
2626 Union Ave.
San Jose, CA 95124

Byte Shop
1225 Ocean St.
Santa Cruz, CA 95060

Byte Shop
1261 Birchwood Dr.
Sunnyvale, CA 94086

Byte Shop
1555 Morse Ave.
Ventura, CA 93003

Byte Shop
1989 North Main St.
Walnut Creek, CA 94596

Byte Shop of Burbank
1812 West Burbank Blvd.
Burbank, CA 94703

Byte Shop of Long Beach
5453 East Stearns St.
Long Beach, CA 90815

Byte Shop of Palo Alto
2227 El Camino Real
Palo Alto, CA 94306

Byte Shop of Placentia
123 East Yorba Linda Blvd.
Placentia, CA 92570

Byte Shop of Sacramento
6041 Greenback Lane
Citrus Heights, CA 95610

Byte Shop of San Francisco
1093 Mission St.
San Francisco, CA 94306

Byte Shop of San Jose
155 Blossom Hill Rd.
San Jose, CA 95123

Byte Shop of San Rafael
509 Francisco Blvd.
San Rafael, CA 94901

Byte Shop of Santa Clara
3400 El Camino Real
Santa Clara, CA 95050

Byte Thousand Oaks
2705 Thousand Oaks Blvd.
Thousand Oaks, CA 91360

Byte Westminster
14300 Beach Blvd.
Westminster, CA 92683

Cabrillo Computer Center
4350 Constellation Dr.
Lompoc, CA 93436

California State University
Student Bookstore
Chico, CA 95926

Century Electronics
447 Associated Rd.
Brea, CA 92621

Channel Radio & Electronics
18 East Ortega St.
Santa Barbara, CA 93101

Computer Center
1913 Harbor Blvd.
Costa Mesa, CA 92627

Computer Center
8205 Ronson Rd.
San Diego, CA 92111

Computer Components
5848 Sepulveda Blvd.
Van Nuys, CA 91411

Computer Country
2232 Salt Air Dr.
Santa Ana, CA 92705

Computer Kits
1044 University Ave.
Berkeley, CA 94710

Computerland
6743 Dublin Blvd.
Dublin, CA 94566

Computerland
11074 San Pablo Ave.
El Cerrito, CA 94530

Computer Land
22634 Foothill Blvd.
Hayward, CA 94541

Computerland
24001 Via Fabricante
Mission Viejo, CA 92675

Computerland
4233 Convoy St.
San Diego, CA 92111

Computerland
117 Fremont St.
San Francisco, CA 94105

Computerland
42–42nd Ave.
San Mateo, CA 94403

Computerland
El Cid Plaza
171 East Thousand Oaks Blvd.
Thousand Oaks, CA 91360

Computerland
104 West 1st St.
Tustin, CA 92680

Computer Mart
625 West Katella No. 10
Orange, CA 92667

Computer Playground
6789 Westminster Ave.
Westminster, CA 92683

Computer Power
Box 28193
San Diego, CA 92128

Computer Power & Light Co.
12321 Ventura Blvd.
Studio City, CA 91604

Computer Room of San Jose
124-H Blossom Hill Rd.
San Jose, CA 95123

Computers & Stuff
664 Via Alamo
San Lorenzo, CA 94580

Computer Shack
Headquarters
14860 Wicks Blvd.
San Leandro, CA 94577

Computer Store
820 Broadway
Santa Monica, CA 90401

Computer Store of San Francisco
1093 Mission St.
San Francisco, CA 94103

Computer Systems Unlimited
18886 Hesperian Blvd.
San Lorenzo, CA 94580

Computerware
830 First St.
Encinitas, CA 92024

Computer Way, Inc.
15525 Computer Lane
Huntington Beach, CA 92649

Computerworld Store
1309 Court Street
Redding, CA 96001

Coyote Computer
1405 Alder Pl.
Davis, CA 95616

CTI Data Systems
3450 East Spring St.
Long Beach, CA 90806

Cyberdux
Microcomputer Applications
1210 Santa Fe Dr.
Encinitas, CA 92024

Data Center
136 North Maryland Ave.
Glendale, CA 91206

DCI Computer Systems
4670 North El Capitan
Fresno, CA 93711

Electric Brain
3038 North Cedar Ave.
Fresno, CA 93703

Electric Brain Computer Store
700 Village Parkway, Suite 1
Dublin, CA 94566

Electronics Plus
823 Fourth St.
San Rafael, CA 94901

Electronics Warehouse, Inc.
1603 Aviation Blvd.
Redondo Beach, CA 90278

Industrial Electronic Control
1304 West St.
Redding, CA 96001

Integrated Circuits Unlimited
7895 Clairemont Mesa Blvd.
San Diego, CA 92111

Itty Bitty Computers
Box 23189
San Jose, CA 95153

Jade Co.
5351 West 144th St.
Lawndale, CA 90260

Kentucky Fried Computers
2465 Fourth St.
Berkeley, CA 94710

Levity Distributors
12010 Dehougne
N. Hollywood, CA 91605

Marketing Director
Computer Country
506 East First St.
Tustin, CA 92680

Melvin Norell
Data Center Store
136 North Maryland Ave.
Glendale, CA 91206

Micro Byte
584 Rio Linda, Suite 4
Chico, CA 95926

Micro Byte
183 East 8th
Chico, CA 95926

Micro Computer Application System
2322 Capitol Ave.
Sacramento, CA 95816

Micro Computers
18120 Brookhurst St.
Fountain Valley, CA 92708

Mission Control
2008 Wilshire Blvd.
Santa Monica, CA 90403

Opamp-Technical Books
1033 North Sycamore Ave.
Los Angeles, CA 90038

People's Computer Shop
13452 Ventura Blvd.
Sherman Oaks, CA 91423

Personal Computer Center
Freeman Engineering
210 Avenue I, Suite C
Redondo Beach, CA 90277

Quement Electronics
1000 South Bascom Ave.
P.O. Box 6000
San Jose, CA 95150

Rainbow Enterprises
10723 White Oak Ave.
Granada Hills, CA 91344

Recreational Computer Centers
1324 South Mary Ave.
P.O. Box 60637
Sunnyvale, CA 94087

Robert Purser
Action Audio Electronics
323 South Mayfair Ave.
Daly City, CA 94015

Small Business Computer Co.
400 Dewey Blvd.
San Francisco, CA 94116

Strawberry Electronics
71 Glenway #9
Belmont, CA 94002

Sunnysounds
927 East Las Tunas Dr.
San Gabriel, CA 91776

Sunny Trading Co.
2530 West Sepulveda Blvd.
Torrance, CA 90505

Sunshine Computer Co.
9 Palomino Lane
Carson, CA 90745

The Byte Shop
1122 B Street
Hayward, CA 94541

The Computer Land
6840 La Cienega Blvd.
Inglewood, CA 90302

Ximedia
1290 24th Ave.
San Francisco, CA 94122

Zackit/Vallejo
1815 Sonoma Blvd.
Vallejo, CA 94590

COLORADO

Byte Colorado
3464 S. Acoma
Englewood, CO 80110

Byte Shop
3101 Walnut Street
Boulder, CO 80301

Computer Country
18 Alameda Square
2200 West Alameda
Denver, CO 80223

Computer Hut
1764 Blake St.
Denver, CO 80202

Gateway Electronics
2839 West 44th Ave.
Denver, CO 80211

Intermountain Digital
1027 Dellwood Ave.
Boulder, CO 80302

J. B. Saunders Co.
3050 Valmont Rd.
Boulder, CO 80301

Team Electronics
3275 28th St.
Boulder, CO 80301

Team Electronics
The Citadel
Colorado Springs, CO 80909

Team Electronics
107 South College
Fort Collins, CO 80521

Team Electronics
Teller Arms Shopping Center
2401 North Ave.
Grand Junction, CO 81051

Team Electronics
1450 Main St.
Longmont, CO 80501

Team Electronics
1022 Constitution Rd.
Belmont Plaza
Pueblo, CO 81001

CONNECTICUT

Computerland
2475 Black Rock Turnpike
Fairfield, CT 06430

Computer Mart
c/o Office Services of Hamden
965 Dixwell Ave.
Hamden, CT 06514

Computer Store Inc.
63 South Main St.
Windsor Locks, CT 06096

Computer World
3876 Main Street
Bridgeport, CT 06606

Heuristic Systems
244 Crystal Lake Rd.
Ellington, CT 06029

JRV Computer Store
3714 Whitney Ave.
Hamden, CT 06518

DELAWARE

Computerland
Astro Shopping Center
Kirkwood Highway
Newark, DE 19711

Delaware Microsystems
92 East Main St. #1
Newark, DE 19711

Drake & Assoc.
1203 Flint Hill Rd.
Wilmington, DE 19808

FLORIDA

Byte Shop
1044 East Oakland Park Blvd.
Ft. Lauderdale, FL 33334

Byte Shop
7825 Bird Road
Miami, FL 33155

Clarks Out of Town News
4 Wall Street
Ft. Lauderdale, FL 33301

Comp Shop
121 East 5th Ave.
Tallahassee, FL 32303

Computer Age
999 Southwest 40th Ave.
Plantation, FL 33317

Computer Associates Inc.
6900 North Kendall Dr., Suite A103
Miami, FL 33156

Computer Hut
6737 Red Rd.
Hialeah, FL 33012

Computer Mart of Florida
4981 72nd Ave. North
Pinellas Park, FL 33565

Computer Store
c/o Comprehensive Systems
P.O. Box 21
Pensacola, FL 32502

Data Entry Engineering
1810 North Orange Ave.
Orlando, FL 32804

Douglas Computer Systems
710 Oaks Plantation Dr.
Jacksonville, FL 32211

Electronic Equipment Co.
4027 Northwest 24th St.
Miami, FL 33142

Marsh Data Systems
5405-B Southern Comfort Blvd.
Tampa, FL 33614

Microcomputer Systems, Inc.
144 South Dale Mabry Highway
Tampa, FL 33609

Micro Computer System Sales &
    Service
P.O. Box 4489
Pompano Beach, FL 33606

Nichols and Assoc.
796 Navy St., Room 112
Ft. Walton Beach, FL 32548

Sunny Computer Stores
University Shopping Center
1238 A S. Dixie Highway
Coral Gables, FL 33146

Sunny Computer Stores
117 Newton Rd.
West Hollywood, FL 33023

Williams Radio & TV
2062 Liberty St.
P.O. Box 3314
Jacksonville, FL 32206

GEORGIA

Altair Software Distribution Center
3330 Peachtree NE, Suite 343
Atlanta, GA 30305

Atlanta Computer Mart
5091-B Buford Highway
Atlanta, GA 30340

Computer Systemcenter
3330 Piedmont Rd. NE
Atlanta, GA 30305

Data Mart
3001 North Fulton Drive
Atlanta, GA 30354

HAWAII

Mahalo Microsystems
Box 8523
Waikiki, HI 96815

Microcomputer Systems of Hawaii
Box 25095
Honolulu, HI 96825

Radio Shack
Pearlridge Shopping Center
Aiea, HI 96701

Real Share
190 South King Street #890
Honolulu, HI 96813

ILLINOIS

Altair Chicago Computer Store
517 Talcott Rd.
Park Ridge, IL 60068

Altair Computer Center
4919 B. North Sheridan Rd.
Peoria, IL 61614

American Microprocessors
241 Indian Creek Rd.
Prairie View, IL 60069

Andich Bros. News Co.
2115 Fourth Ave.
Rock Island, IL 61201

Aspen Computers
7521 West Irving Pk. Rd.
Chicago, IL 60634

Bits and Bytes Computer Shop
2928 West 147th St.
Posen, IL 60469

Byte Shop
5 South La Grange Rd.
La Grange, IL 60525

Champaign Computer Co.
318 North Neil St.
Champaign, IL 61820

Chicago Computer Store
One Illinois Center
Chicago, IL 60601

Chicago Computer Store
517 Talcott Rd.
Park Ridge, IL 60068

Computerland
9511 North Milwaukee Rd.
Niles, IL 60648

Computerland
10935 South Cicero Ave.
Oak Lawn, IL 60453

Data Domain
42 West Roosevelt
Lombard, IL 60148

George Electronics, Inc.
325 East 147th St.
Harvey, IL 60426

Itty-Bitty Machine Co.
1318 Chicago Ave.
Evanston, IL 60201

Joseph Electronics
1733 North Harlem Ave.
Chicago, IL 60635

Joseph Electronics, Inc.
8830 North Milwaukee Ave.
Niles, IL 60648

MPU Shop
c/o Semiconductor Specialists
195 Spangler Ave.
Elmhurst, IL 60126

Midwest Micro Computers, Inc.
708 South Main
Lombard, IL 60148

Midwest System Group, Inc.
413 Wrightwood Ave.
Elmhurst, IL 60126

Team Electronics
Meadowdale Dr., Space 1A
Carpentersville, IL 60110

Team Electronics
Northgate Mall Shopping Ctr.
Decatur, IL

Team Electronics
Sandburg Mall
1150 West Carl Sandburg Drive
Galesburg, IL 61401

Team Electronics
Southpark Shopping Center
4200 16th Street
Moline, IL 61265

Team Electronics
4700 Block North University Ave.
Peoria, IL 61614

Team Electronics
321 North Alpine Rd.
Rockford, IL 61107

Team Electronics
1714 5th Ave.
Rock Island, IL 61201

Team Electronics
Woodfield Mall F 119
Schaumburg, IL 60172

Team Electronics
2716 South MacArthur Blvd.
Springfield, IL 62704

INDIANA

Byte Shope of Indianapolis
5947 East 82 St.
Indianapolis, IN 46250

Data Domain
111 South College Ave.
Bloomington, IN 47401

Data Domain
7027 Michigan Rd. North
Indianapolis, IN 46268

Hobbytronic Distributors
1218 Prairie Dr.
Bloomington, IN 47401

Quantum Computer Works
6637 Kennedy Ave.
Hammond, IN 46323

IOWA

Micro Computer Store
328 Grand Ave.
West Des Moines, IA 50265

Radio Trade Supply Co.
1017 High St.
Des Moines, IA 50309

Team Electronics
202 Main Street
Ames, IA 50010

Team Electronics
Duck Creek Plaza
Bettendorf, IA 52722

Team Electronics
4444 First Ave. NE
Lindale Plaza
Cedar Rapids, IA 52401

Team Electronics
920 Kimberly Road
Northpark Shopping Center
Davenport, IA 52806

Team Electronics
2300 Kennedy Road
Dubuque, IA 52001

Team Electronics
Room 120 Space 18
The Mall
Iowa City, IA 52240

Team Electronics
2015 East Fourth
Sioux City, IA 50313

Team Electronics
KD Stockyards Station
2001 Leech Ave.
Sioux City, IA 51107

Team Electronics
2750 University Ave.
Waterloo, IA 50701

The Computer Store of
    Davenport
4128 Brady
Davenport, IA 52806

KANSAS

Amateur Radio Equipment Co.
1203 East Douglas
Wichita, KS 67211

Barney and Assoc.
425 North Broadway
Rittsburg, KS

Computer Center
5815 Johnson Dr.
Mission, KS 66202

Computer Land
1262 North Hillside
Wichita, KS 67214

Computer Systems Design
1611 East Central
Wichita, KS 67214

Midwest Scientific Instruments,
    Inc.
220 West Cedar
Olathe, KS 66061

Team Electronics
215 West Kansas Ave.
Garden City, KS 67846

Team Electronics
14 South Main St.
Hutchinson, KS 67501

Team Electronics
Space 81-A Mid-State Mall
Salina, KS 67401

Team Electronics
2319 Louisiana St.
Lawrence, KS 66044

Team Electronics
1132 Westloop Shopping Center
Manhattan, KS 66502

Team Electronics
The Mall on Harry Street
Wichita, KS

Team Electronics
907 West 27th St. Terrace
Topeka, KS 66614

Team Electronics
Towne East Square
7700 East Kellogg
Wichita, KS 67207

KENTUCKY

Computerland
813-B Lyndon Lane
Louisville, KY 40222

Cybertronics
312 Production Court
Louisville, KY 40299

Data Domain
506 ½ Euclid Ave.
Lexington, KY 40502

Data Domain
3028 Hunsinger Lane
Louisville, KY 40220

Logic Systems
324 West Woodlawn Ave.
Louisville, KY 40214

LOUISIANA

Computer Shoppe, Inc.
3828 Veterans Blvd., Suite 200
Metairie, LA 70002

Davis Wholesale Electronics
3575 Choctaw Dr.
Baton Rouge, LA 70805

Executone Microcomputer
6969 Titian Ave.
Baton Rouge, LA 70806

Val Coor
Computer Electronics
1986 Bequmont Dr.
Baton Rouge, LA 70806

MARYLAND

Computer Workshop
11308 Hounds Way
Rockville, MD 20852

Computer Workshop
5709 Frederick Ave.
Rockville, MD 20852

Computer Workshop of Baltimore
4005 Seven Mile Lane
Baltimore, MD 21208

MASSACHUSETTS

American Used Computer
712 Beacon St.
Boston, MA 02215

American Used Computer
 Warehouse Store
584 Commonwealth Ave.
Boston, MA 02215

Bob Rivers
Computer Shop, Div. Aircom
288 Norfack St.
Cambridge, MA 02139

Central Concepts
Box 272
Needham Heights, MA 02194

Computer Mart, Inc.
1097 Lexington St.
Waltham, MA 02154

Computer Mart
473 Winter St.
Waltham, MA 02154

Computer Store Inc.
120 Cambridge
Burlington, MA 01803

MICHIGAN

Compumart, Inc.
254 South Wagner Rd.
Ann Arbor, MI 48103

Computerland
2927 28th St.
Kentwood, MI 94508

Computer Mart, Inc.
1800 West 14 Mile Rd.
Royal Oak, MI 48073

Computer Mart of Royal Oak
1800 West 14 Michigan Rd.
Royal Oak, MI 48073

Computer Store of Ann Arbor
310 East Washington St.
Ann Arbor, MI 48104

General Computer Co.
420 Main Street
Brighton, MI 48084

General Computer Store
1310 Michigan Ave.
East Lansing, MI 48823

Newman Computer Exchange
1250 North Main Street
Ann Arbor, MI 48104

Team Electronics
Delta Plaza Shopping Center
Escanaba, MI

Team Electronics
Mand M Plaza
Menominee, MI

The General Computer Co.
2017 Livernois
Troy, MI 48084

MINNESOTA

Byte Minnesota, Inc.
1434 Yankee Doodle Rd.
Eagan, MN 55122

Computer Depot, Inc.
3515 West 70th
Minneapolis, MN 55435

Computer Room
3938 Beau D'Rue Dr.
Eagan, MN 55122

Team Electronics
207 Third
Bemidji, MN 56601

Team Electronics
1248 Eden Prairie Center
Eden Prairie, MN 55343

Team Electronics
204 Southdale Center
Edina, MN 55435

Team Electronics
310 Grant
Eveleth, MN 55734

Team Electronics
Mesabi Mall
Hibbing, MN 55746

Team Electronics
Madison East
Mankato, MN 56001

Team Electronics
Maplewood Plaza
30000 Whitebear Ave.
Maplewood, MN 55109

Team Electronics
1311 Fourth St. SE
Minneapolis, MN 55810

Team Electronics
2640 Hennepin Ave. South
Minneapolis, MN 55408

Team Electronics
6314 Lindale Ave. South
Minneapolis, MN

Team Electronics
Ridgedale Mall
12503 Wayzata Blvd.
Minnetonka, MN 55343

Team Electronics
Cedar Mall
Owatonna, MN 55060

Team Electronics
Apache Plaza
Silver Lake Rd.
St. Anthony, MN 55414

Team Electronics
110 Sixth Ave. South
St. Cloud, MN 56301

Team Electronics
Crossroads Shopping Center
St. Cloud, MN 56301

Team Electronics
Har Mar Mall
St. Paul, MN 55113

Team Electronics
455 Rice
St. Paul, MN 55103

Team Electronics
Thunderbird Mall
Virginia, MN 55792

Team Electronics
1733 South Robert Rd.
West St. Paul, MN 55118

Team Electronics
Kandi Mall
South Highway 71
Wilmar, MN 56201

MISSOURI

Computer Workshop, Inc.
  of Kansas City
6903 Blair Rd.
Kansas City, MO 64152

Electronic Components Intl.
1306 South B Highway 63
Columbia, MO 65201

Gateway Electronics
8123-25 Page Blvd.
St. Louis, MO 63130

Micro-Com, Inc.
6314 Brookside Plaza
Suite 202
Kansas City, MO 64113

Team Electronics
Biscayne Mall
301 Stadium Blvd.
Columbia, MO 65201

The Computer Workshop of K.C.
6903 Blair Rd.
Kansas City, MO 64152

MONTANA

Computers Made Easy
415 Morrow
Bozeman, MT 59715

Montana Computer Center
2512 Grand Ave.
Billings, MT 59102

Team Electronics
612 Central Ave.
Great Falls, MT 59401

Team Electronics
1208 West Kent
Missoula, MT 59801

NEBRASKA

Altair Computer Center
2810 Cornhusker Highway
Lincoln, NB 68504

Altair Computer Center
611 North 47th St., Suite 9
Lincoln, NB 68503

Omaha Computer Store
4540 South 84th St.
Omaha, NB 68127

Team Electronics
148 Conestoga Mall
Highway 281 and 13th
Grand Island, NB 68801

Team Electronics
2055 O St.
Lincoln, NB 68510

Team Electronics
Sunset Plaza
Norfolk, NB 68701

Team Electronics
The Mall
1000 South Dewey
North Platte, NB 69101

Team Electronics
Bel Air Plaza
12100 West Center Rd.
Omaha, NB 68503

Team Electronics
Cedarnole Shopping Ctr.
Omaha, NB

Welling Electronics
529 North 33rd St.
Omaha, NB 68131

NEW HAMPSHIRE

Computerland
419 Amherst
Nashua, NH 03060

Computer Mart of New Hampshire
170 Main St.
Nashua, NH 03060

Micro Computers Inc.
539 Amherst St.
Nashua, NH 03060

World Wide Electronics, Inc.
10 Flagstone Dr.
Hudson, NH 03051

NEW JERSEY

Computerland
2 De Hart St.
Morristown, NJ 07960

Computer Mart of New Jersey, Inc.
501 Route 27
Iselin, NJ 08830

Computer Room
451 Simons Ave.
Hackensack, NJ 07601

Hoboken Computer Works
20 Hudson Place
Hoboken, NJ 07030

Midwest Enterprises Inc.
815 Standish Ave.
Westfield, NJ 07090

William Electronics Supply
1863 Woodbridge Ave.
Edison, NJ 08817

NEW MEXICO

Computer Shack
3120 San Mateo NE
Albuquerque, NM 87110

Electronic Parts Co.
2620 Rhode Island NE
Albuquerque, NM 87110

NEW YORK

Apex Electronics
141 Northwood Ave.
West Seneca, NY 14224

Byte Long Island N.Y.
2721 Hempstead Turnpike
Levittown, NY 11756

Central N.Y. Computer Shop
3307 Erie Blvd. East
DeWitt, NY 13214

Command Electronics Corp.
114 Allen Blvd.
Farmingdale, NY 11735

Computer Corner
200 Hamilton Ave.
White Plains, NY 10013

Computer Mart of Long Island, Inc.
2072 Front St.
East Meadow, NY 11554

Computer Mart of New York
314 Fifth Ave.
New York, NY 10001

Computer Mart of New York
118 Madison Ave.
New York, NY 10010

Computer Microsystems
6 Wooleys Lane
Great Neck, NY 11023

Computer Microsystems
1311 Northern Blvd.
Manhasset, NY 11023

Computer Store
269 Osborne Rd.
Albany, NY 12211

Computer Store of New York
55 West 39th St.
New York, NY 10018

Computer Tree, Inc.
409 Hooper Rd.
Endwell, NY 13760

Computerland
1612 Niagara Falls Blvd.
Buffalo, NY 14150

Computerland
225 Elmira Rd.
Ithaca, NY 14850

Comput-O-Mat-Systems
41 Colby Ave.
Rye, NY 10580

Co-Op Electronics
9148 Main
Clarence, NY 14031

Harrison Radio Corp.
20 Smith St.
Farmingdale, NY 11735

Hirsh Sales Co.
219 California Drive
Williamsville, NY 14221

Memory Merchants
1350 Buffalo Road
Rochester, NY 14624

Microcomputer Workshop
234 Tennyson Terrace
Williamsville, NY 14221

MJB Research & Development
36 West 62nd St.
New York, NY 10023

Rochester Radio Supply Co.
140 West Main
Rochester, NY 14603

Synchro Sound Enterprises
193–25 Jamaica Ave.
Hollis, NY 11423

The Computer Shoppe
444 Middle Country Rd.
Middle Island, NY 11953

NORTH CAROLINA

Altair Computer Center
1808 East Independence
Charlotte, NC 28205

Byte Shop
1213 Hillsborough St.
Raleigh, NC 27605

Computerroom
1729 Garden Terrace
Charlotte, NC 28203

ROMs 'N' RAMs
Crabtree Valley Mall
Raleigh, NC 27604

NORTH DAKOTA

Team Electronics
2304 East Broadway
Bismark, ND 58501

Team Electronics
West Acres Shopping Ctr.
Fargo, ND 58102

Team Electronics
1503 11th Ave. North
Grand Forks, ND 58201

Team Electronics
209 11th Ave. SW
Minot, ND 58701

Team Electronics
109 Main
Williston, ND 58801

OHIO

Altair Computer Center
45 Murray Hill Dr.
Dayton, OH 45403

Byte Shop
2432 Chester Lane
Columbus, OH 43321

Cincinnati Computer Store
9195 Reading Rd. at Columbia Ave.
Cincinnati, OH 45215

Computer Mart of Dayton
2665 South Dixie
Dayton, OH 45409

Computerland
1304 SOM Center Rd.
Mayfield Heights, OH 44124

Computerland of Cleveland East
2136 Lyndway Rd.
Beachwood, OH 44122

Cybershop
1451 South Hamilton Rd.
Columbus, OH 43227

E. L. S. Systems Engineering
Small Computer Store
2209 North Taylor
Cleveland Heights, OH 44112

Ridgeway East
Retail Computer Center
161 Bell St.
Chagrin Falls, OH 44022

The Data Domain
1932 Brown St.
Dayton, OH 45409

The Sun Radio Co.
P.O. Box 390
Akron, OH 44308

21st Century Shop
4040 Beachwood Ave.
Cincinnati, OH 45229

21st Century Shop
16 Convention Way
Cincinnati, OH 45202

Winterradio Electronic Supply Corp.
1468 West 25th St.
Cleveland, OH 44113

OKLAHOMA

Altair Computer Ctr.
110 The Annex
5345 East 41st Street
Tulsa, OK 74135

Bits, Bytes & Micros
1186 North MacArthur Blvd.
Oklahoma City, OK 73127

Derrick Electronics
P.O. Box 457
Broken Arrow, OK 74012

Global Engineering Co.
5416 South Yale
Tulsa, OK 74145

High Technology
1020 West Wilshire Blvd.
Oklahoma City, OK 74116

Team Electronics
1105 Elm
Stubbman Village
Norman, OK 73069

Team Electronics
Penn Square Shopping Ctr.
Oklahoma City, OK

Team Electronics
7000 Crossroads 32010
Oklahoma City, OK 73149

Team Electronics
1134 Hall of Fame
Stilwell, OK 74960

Team Electronics
5305 East 41st
Tulsa, OK 74135

Team Electronics
7021 Memorial
Tulsa, OK 74125

Team Electronics
Surrey Hills
Yukon, OK 73099

University Center Bookstore
Central St. University
Edmond, OK 73034

OREGON

Altair Computer Center
8105 Southwest Nimbus Ave.
Beaverton, OR 97005

Byte Shop Computer Store
3482 Southwest Cedar Hills Blvd.
Beaverton, OR 97401

Computer Pathways Unlimited
145 Alice St. SE
Salem, OR 97302

Real Oregon Computer Co.
205 West 10th Ave.
Eugene, OR 97401

Team Electronics
1913 Northeast Third
Bend, OR 97701

Team Electronics
1023 Southwest First
Canby, OR 97013

Team Electronics
2230 Fairground Rd. NE
Salem, OR 97303

PENNSYLVANIA

Artco Electronics
302 Wyoming Ave.
Kingston, PA 18704

Artco Electronics
Back Mountain Shopping Center
Shavertown, PA 18708

Byte Philadelphia
1045 West Lancaster Ave.
Bryn Mawr, PA 19010

Caldwell Computer Co.
546 West Olney Ave.
Philadelphia, PA 19120

Computer Room
c/o Carol Groves Castle Systems
1028 Spruce St.
Philadelphia, PA 19107

Computer Workshop of Pittsburgh
4170 William Penn Highway
Murraysville, PA 15668

J. B. Industries
610 West Olney Ave.
Philadelphia, PA 19120

Marketline Systems
2337 Philmont
Huntingdon Valley, PA 19006

Martin J. O'Boyle & Assoc.
Box 9094
Pittsburgh, PA 15224

Personal Computer Corp.
Frazer Mall
Frazer, PA 19355

RHODE ISLAND

Computer Power Inc.
M24 Airport Mall
1800 Post Rd.
Warwick, RI 02886

SOUTH CAROLINA

Byte Shop
2018 Green St.
Columbia, SC 29205

World of Computers
5849 Dorchester Rd.
Charleston Heights, SC 29405

SOUTH DAKOTA

Team Electronics
402 West Sioux Ave.
Pierre, SD 57501

Team Electronics
1101 Omaha St.
Rapid City, SD 57701

Team Electronics
613 West 41st
Sioux Falls, SD 57105

Team Electronics
41st and Western
Sioux Falls, SD

Team Electronics
Sioux Empire Mall
4001 West 41st
Sioux Falls, SD 57106

Team Electronics
223 Ninth Ave.
Watertown, SD 57201

TENNESSEE

Byte 'Tronics
1600 Hayes St.,
Suite 103
Nashville, TN 37203

Computer Den
1507-A Oak Ridge Turnpike
Oak Ridge, TN 37830

Docs Computer Shop
5755 Nolensville Rd.
Nashville, TN 37211

Microproducts and Systems
2307 East Center
Kingsport, TN 37664

Tobacco Corner Newsroom
671 South Mendhalle
Memphis, TN 38117

TEXAS

Altair Computer Center
12902 Harwin
Houston, TX 77072

Byte Shop
3211 Fondren
Houston, TX 77042

City Electronic Supply
5074 Richmond Ave.
Houston, TX 77056

Computer Mart of West Texas
3506-D Ave. Q
Lubbock, TX 79412

Computer Port
926 North Collins
Arlington, TX 76011

Computer Store
3801 Kirbey #432
Houston, TX 77098

Computer Stores, Inc.
13933 North Central
Dallas, TX 75231

Computerland
Shoal Creek Plaza
3300 Anderson Lane
Austin, TX 78757

Computerland
6439 Westheimer Rd.
Houston, TX 77057

Computer Terminal
2101 Myrtle
El Paso, TX 79901

Computertex
2300 Richmond Ave.
Houston, TX 77006

Digitex
2111 Farrington St.
Dallas, TX 75207

Electrotex
2300 Richmond Ave.
Houston, TX 66907

Houston Computer Mart
8027 Gulf Freeway
Houston, TX 77017

Interactive Computers
P.O. Box 36584
Houston, TX 77036

Interactive Computers
7646 ½ Dashwood Rd.
Houston, TX 77036

K. A. Electronic Sales
1220 Majesty Dr.
Dallas, TX 75247

Mr. Calculator
2 Shell Plaza
777 Walker
Houston, TX 77002

Neighborhood Computer Store
#20 Terrace Shopping Ctr.
4902 34th St.
Lubbock, TX 79412

The Micro Store
634 South Central Expressway
Richardson, TX 75080

Polaris Computer Systems
3311 Richmond Station 200
Houston, TX 77006

Southwest Technical Products
219 West Rhapsody
San Antonio, TX 78216

Tanner Electronics
11423 Harry Hines Blvd.
Dallas, TX 75229

The Computer Shop
6812 San Pedro
San Antonio, TX 78216

UTAH

Byte Shop
261 South State
Salt Lake City, UT 84111

Central Utah Electronics Supply
P.O. Box N
Provo, UT 84601

Computer Room
1455 South 1100 East
Salt Lake City, UT 84105

Computer Room
3455 Southwest Temple St.
Salt Lake City, UT 84115

VIRGINIA

Arcade Electronics, Inc.
7048 Columbia Pike
Annandale, VA 22003

Computer Hobbies Unlimited
9601 Kendrick Rd.
Richmond, VA 23235

Computer Workshop of N.V.
5240 Port Royal RD No. 203
Springfield, VA 22151

Computers To Go
1905 Westmoreland St.
Richmond, VA 23230

Media Reactions, Inc.
11800 Sunrise Reston Ctr.
Valley Drive Suite #312
Reston, VA 22091

Microsystems
6605-A Blacklick Rd.
Springfield, VA

The Computer Systems Store
1984 Chain Bridge Rd.
McLean, VA 22101

The Home Computer Co.
Box 1891
University Station
Charlottesville, VA 22903

Timberville Electronics
Box 202
Timberville, VA 22853

WASHINGTON

Almac-Stroum
5811 Sixth Ave. South
Seattle, WA 98108

Byte Shop Computer Store
14701 Northeast 20th Ave.
Bellevue, WA 98007

Microcomputer Applications
6009-B 13th Way SE
Olympia, WA 98503

Pacific Computer Store
Northern Communications
410 West Champion St.
Bellingham, WA 98225

Personal Computers
Suite 101A Tapio Office Center
104 Freya St.
Spokane, WA 99202

Retailer Computer Store
410 Northeast 72nd
Seattle, WA 98115

Team Electronics
423 West Yakima
Yakima, WA 98902

WISCONSIN

Altair Computer Store
285 West Northland Ave.
Appleton, WI 54911

Itty Bitty Machine Co.
2221 East Capitol Dr.
Shorewood, WI 53211

Leonard Lindsay, Manager
The Computer Shop
5406 Flad Ave.
Madison, WI 53711

Madison Computer Store
1863 Monroe Street
Madison, WI 53711

Milwaukee Computer Store
6916 West North Ave.
Milwaukee, WI 53213

Team Electronics
3365 East Clairmont Pky.
Eau Claire, WI 54701

Team Electronics
3209 Rudolph Rd.
Eau Claire, WI 54701

Team Electronics
5300 South 76
Southridge Ctr.
Greendale, WI 53129

Team Electronics
2619 Milton Ave.
Janesville, WI 53545

Team Electronics
1505 Losey Blvd. South
La Crosse, WI 54601

Team Electronics
3365 East Washington
Madison, WI 53704

Team Electronics
1801 Marshall St.
Manitowoc, WI 54220

Team Electronics
7700 West Brown Deer Road
Milwaukee, WI 53223

Team Electronics
7512 West Appleton
Milwaukee, WI 53216

Team Electronics
3301-3500 South 27th
Milwaukee, WI 53215

Team Electronics
396 Park Ave.
Oshkosh, WI 54901

Team Electronics
3701 Durand
Elmwood Plaza Shopping Ctr.
Racine, WI 53405

Team Electonics
Sunrise Plaza
Rhinelander, WI 54501

Team Electronics
3347 Kohler Ave.
Memorial Hall No. 4
Sheboygan, WI 53081

Team Electronics
2207 Grand Ave.
Wausau, WI 54401

WEST VIRGINIA

Computer Store
1114 Charleston National Plaza
Charleston, WV 25301

Radio Shack
211 Dickinson
Charleston, WV 25301

WYOMING

Team Electronics
207 South Montana
Casper, WY 82601

FOREIGN

Computerland
52–58 Clarence St.
Sydney, N.S.W.
Australia

CANADA

Basic Computer Group
1438 East 8th
Vancouver, B.C.

Byte Shop
665 Century St.
Winnipeg, Man.

Computer Mart
1543 Bayview
Toronto, Ont.

Computer Place
186 Queen St. West
Toronto, Ont.

First Canadian Computer Store
44 Eglinton Ave. West
Toronto, Ont.

Future Byte
2274 Rockland
Montreal, Que.

Orothon Computers
12411 Stony Plain Road
Edmonton, Alberta T5N 3N3

Pacific Computer Store
4509 Rupert
Vancouver, B.C.

Trintronics
160 Elgin
Ottawa, Ont.

APPENDIX B:
COMPUTER COMPANIES

One of the best ways to get information on computer products is to write directly to the factory and ask for catalogs and brochures. The following list is included so that you can do just that. It is not complete and some addresses may change.

Advanced Micro Devices
901 Thompson Place
Sunnyvale, CA 94086

Advanced Microcomputer Products
Box 17329
Irvine, CA 92713

Anderson Jacobson, Inc.
521 Charcat Ave.
San Jose, CA 95131

Apple Computer
348 Waverly St.
Palo Alto, CA 94301

Artec Electronics
20863 Stevens Creek Blvd.
Cupertino, CA 95014

Atari
1265 Barregas Ave.
Sunnyvale, CA 94086

Bally Consumer Products Division
10750 West Grand Ave.
Franklin Park, IL 60131

Basic Four Corp.
2015 Spring Rd., Suite 125
Oakbrook, IL 60521

California Business Machines
2211 The Alameda
Santa Clara, CA 95050

Champaign Computer, Co.
Box 1524
Champaign, IL 61820

Coleco Industries
945 Asylum Ave.
Hartford, CT 06105

Commodore Business Machines
901 California Ave.
Palo Alto, CA 94304

Comptek Real World Electronics
P.O. Box 516
La Canada, CA 91011

Compucolor Corp.
1422 West Peachtree Northwest
Atlanta, GA 30309

Computer Automation, Inc.
18651 Von Karmon
Irvine, CA 92664

Computer Company, Inc.
5849 Dorchester Rd.
Charleston Heights, SC 29405

Computer Devices, Inc.
5901 North Cicero
Chicago, IL 60610

Computer Music, Inc.
Box 27160
Philadelphia, PA 19118

Computer Power & Light
12321 Ventura Blvd.
Studio City, CA 91604

Computer Systems Unlimited
18886 Hesperian Blvd.
Hayward, CA 94541

Computers Unlimited
7724 East 89th St.
Indianapolis, IN 46250

Continental Specialties Corp.
44 Kendall St.
New Haven, CT 06509

Cromemco
2400 Charleston Rd.
Mountain View, CA 94043

Cybercom/Solid State Music
2102A Walsh
Santa Clara, CA 95050

Data Access Systems
201 East Chestnut
Chicago, IL 60611

Data Electronics
4976 Milwaukee Ave.
Chicago, IL 60630

Data General
15 Turnpike Rd.
Westfall, MA 01581

Data Terminals & Communications
1190 Dell Ave.
Campbell, CA 95008

Digital Business Systems
244 Main
Reading, PA 01867

Digital Equipment Corp.
1 Iron Way
Marlboro, MS 01752

Digital Group
P.O. Box 6528
Denver, CO 80206

Digital Systems
1154 Dunsmuir Pl.
Livermore, CA 94550

E & L Instruments
61 First St.
Derby, CT 06418

ECD Corp.
196 Broadway
Cambridge, MA 02139

Electronic Specialties, Inc.
171 South Main St.
Natick, MA 01760

Extensys Corp.
5921 Weddell Dr.
Sunnyvale, CA 94086

Fairchild Consumer Products
4001 Miranda Ave.
Palo Alto, CA 94304

Fidelity Electronics Ltd.
5245 West Diversey
Chicago, IL 60689

GIMIX
1337 West 37th Pl.
Chicago, IL 60609

General Automation
1055 South East St.
Anaheim, CA 92805

Godbout Electronics
Box 2355
Oakland Airport, CA 94614

Hal Communications Corp.
Box 365, 807 East Green St.
Urbana, IL 61801

Harris Corporation
Daniel Webster Hwy. South
Nashua, NH 03060

Heuristics, Inc.
134 Tealwood Dr.
Montgomery, IL 60538

Ibex
1010 Morse Ave., #5
Sunnyvale, CA 94086

Icom Division-Pertec
6741 Variel Ave.
Canoga Park, CA 91303

Imsai
14860 Wicks Blvd.
San Leandro, CA 94577

Info-Tech, Inc.
20 Worthington Dr.
St. Louis, MO 63043

Information Systems, Inc.
704 11th
Wilmette, IL 60091

Information Terminals
323 Soquel Way
Sunnyvale, CA 94086

Intel Corp.
3065 Bowers Ave.
Santa Clara, CA 95051

Intelligent Computer Systems
777 Middlefield Rd., #40
Mt. View, CA 94043

Intersil, Inc.
10900 North Tantau Ave.
Cupertino, CA 95014

J&L Systems, Inc.
282 Weyman Ave.
New Rochelle, NY 10805

Jade Company
5351 West 144 St.
Lawndale, CA 90260

Jámes Computer Co.
4790 North Marine
Chicago, IL 60640

Lear-Siegler
714 North Brookhurst
Anaheim, CA 92803

Lillipute Computer Mart
4460 Oakton
Skokie, IL 60076

Logical Machine Co.
1294 Hammerwood Ave.
Sunnyvale, CA 94086

MBD Systems, Inc.
1995 North Batavia St.
Orange, CA 92665

Micro Designs, Inc.
499 Embacadero
Oakland, CA 94606

Micro Games
10888 North 19th Ave.
Phoenix, AZ 85021

Micro-Term, Inc.
P.O. Box 9387
St. Louis, MO 63117

Microcomputer Associates
Box 1167
Cupertino, CA 95014

Microcomputer Devices
960 East Orangethrope Building 5
Anaheim, CA 92801

Microelectronic Systems Corp.
29245 Stephenson Hwy.
Madison Heights, MI 48071

Micromation, Inc.
524 Union St.
San Francisco, CA 94133

Micropolis Corp.
9017 Reseda Blvd., #204
Northridge, CA 91324

Microsoft
300 San Mateo NE
Suite 819
Albuquerque, NM 87108

Microtronics
Box 7454
Menlo Park, CA 94025

Midwest Scientific Instruments
220 West Cedar
Olathe, KS 66061

Mits, Inc.
2450 Alamo SE
Albuquerque, NM 87106

National Semiconductor
1177 Kearn Ave.
Sunnyvale, CA 94106

National Teletypewriter Corp.
207 Newtown Rd.
Plainview, NY 11803

Network Technology Co.
P.O. Box 145, Prudential Ctr.
Boston, MA 02199

North Star Computers, Inc.
2465 4th St.
P.O. Box 4672
Berkeley, CA 94710

OK Machine & Tool Corp.
3455 Conner St.
Bronx, NY 10475

Ohio Scientific Instruments
11679 Hayden St.
Hiram, OH 44234

Parasitic Engineering
Box 6314 & Box 6194
Albany, CA 94706

Peripheral Vision
P.O. Box 6267
Denver, CO 80206

PerSci
4087 Glencoe Ave.
Marina Del Rey, CA 90291

Polymorphic Systems
737 South Kellog
Goleta, CA 94017

Prime Radix, Inc.
1764 Blake St./80202
Box 11245
Denver, CO 80211

Processor Technology
6200 Hallis St., Box L
Emeryville, CA 94608

RCA Corp.
Solid State Division
Somerville, NJ 08876

Radio Shack
2617 West 7th St.
Fort Worth, TX 76107

Rondure Corp.
2522 Butler
Dallas, TX 75235

S-100, Inc.
7 White Place
Clark, NJ 07066

SD Sales
Box 2810
Dallas, TX 75228

STM Systems, Inc.
P.O. Box 248
Mt. Vernon, NH 03057

Scientific Micro-Systems, Inc.
520 Clyde Ave.
Mountain View, CA 94043

Scientific Programming
2213 Jefferson
Berkeley, CA 94703

Scientific Research, Inc.
1712 Farmington Ct.
Crofton, MD 21114

Seals Electronics
10728 Dutchtown Rd.
Concord, TN 37922

Small Computer Systems Corp.
Box 4344
Warren, NJ 07060

Smoke Signal Broadcasting
Box 2017
Hollywood, CA 90028

Software Magic Co.
11411 Sageking
Houston, TX 77089

Software Records
P.O. Box 8401 B
Universal City, CA 91608

Software Technology Corp.
Box 5260
San Mateo, CA 94402

Solfan System, Inc.
66 South Clyde Ave.
Mt. View, CA 94043

Soroc Tech, Inc.
165 Freedom Ave.
Anaheim, CA 92801

Southwest Technical Products
219 West Rhapsody
San Antonio, TX 78216

Space Byte
2400 Aspen Dr.
Los Angeles, CA 90068

Speech Technology Corp.
631 Wilshire Blvd.
Santa Monica, CA 90401

Sub Logic
Box 3442
Culver City, CA 90230

Sunrise Electronics
228 North El Molino St.
Pasadena, CA 91101

Sunset Technologies
P.O. Box 2411
Goleta, CA 93018

Sunshine Computer Co.
20710 South Leapwood Ave.
Carson, CA 90746

Symbiotic Systems
Rt. 1, Box 266
Woodland, CA 95695

Syncrosound
193–25 Jamaica Ave.
Jamaica, NY 11423

Synetic Designs
1452 Prospect Dr.
Pomona, CA 91766

Szerlip Enterprises
1414 West 259 St.
Harbor City, CA 90710

TCB Corporation
4709 Tecumsen St., #201
College Park, MD 20740

TEC Industries, Inc.
1857 West Maple Rd.
Walled Lake, MI 48088

Tarbell Electronics
144 Miraleste Dr., #106
Miraleste, CA 90733

Technical Design Labs
Bldg. H, 1101 State Road
Princeton, NJ 08540

Teletype Corporation
5555 West Touhy Ave.
Skokie, IL 60076

Texas Instruments
13500 North Central Expressway
Dallas, TX 75231

Vector Graphics, Inc.
717 Lakefield Rd., Suite F
Westlake Village, CA 91361

Vera Systems
P.O. Box 74E
Somerville, MA 02143

Victor Business Products Group
3900 North Rockwell
Chicago, IL 60618

VideoBrain
150 South Wolfe Road
Sunnyvale, CA 94068

Video Terminal Technology
P.O. Box 60485
Sunnyvale, CA 94088

Videodyssey
Lake Cook Plaza
461 Lake Cook Rd.
Deerfield, IL 60015

Wang Laboratories
836 North St.
Tewksbury, MA 01876

Wave-Mate
1015 West 190 St.
Gardena, CA 90248

Western Data Systems
3650 Charles St., #G
Santa Clara, CA 95050

Ximedia
1290 24th Ave.
San Francisco, CA 94122

Xitex
P.O. Box 20887
Dallas, TX 75220

Xybex
P.O. Box 4925
Stanford, CA 94305

APPENDIX C:
COMPUTER CLUBS

Contacting a computer club in your area may be a good way to find out about personal computers. A club may help you meet people whose interests in computing are similar to your own. And many clubs publish informative newsletters that are very worthwhile reading. Again, this list is probably not complete and some of the addresses may have changed.

ALABAMA

North Alabama Computer Club
Jack Crenshaw
1409 Blevins Gap Rd. SE
Huntsville, AL 35802

CALIFORNIA

Bay Area Microprocessors Users
    Group
4565 Black Ave.
Pleasanton, CA 94566

Beverly Hills High School
    Computer Club
241 Marino Dr.
Beverly Hills, CA 90212

Computer Guild
P.O. Box 255232
Sacramento, CA 95825

Computer Organization of Los
    Angeles (COLA)
Box 43677
Los Angeles, CA 90043

Computer Phreaques United
c/o Mac McCormick
2090 Cross St.
Seaside, CA 93955

Glendale Community College
    Computer Club
c/o V. S. Lashleu
1500 North Verdugo Rd.
Glendale, CA 92108

Homebrew Computer Club
P.O. Box 626
Mountain View, CA 94040

HP-65 Users Group
c/o Richard J. Nelson
2541 West Camden Place
Santa Ana, CA 90024

LO*OP Center
8099 La Plaza
Cotati, CA 94928

LLLRA Hobbyist Group
c/o Charles D. Hoover
35 West Essen St.
Stockton, CA 95204

Litton Calculator/Computer
    Club
MS 78/31
5500 Canoga Ave.
Woodland Hills, CA 91364

North Orange County Computer
    Club
Box 3603
Orange, CA 92665

Sacramento Minicomputer Users
    Group
P.O. Box 741
Citrus Heights, CA 95610

San Diego Computing Society
P.O. Box 9988
San Diego, CA 92109

San Gabriel SCCS
c/o Dan Erickson
400 South Catalina Ave.
Pasadena, CA 91106

San Luis Obispo Microcomputer
    Club
439 B. Marsh St.
San Luis Obispo, CA 93401

Santa Barbara Computer Group
c/o Glenn A. McComb
210 Barrunca, Apt. 2
Santa Barbara, CA 93101

Santa Barbara
Nameless Computer Club
c/o Doug Penrod
1445 La Clima Road
Santa Barbara, CA 93101

Southern California Computer
    Society
P.O. Box 987
South Pasadena, CA 91030

Southern California Computer
    Society
P.O. Box 54751
Los Angeles, CA 90054

Technical Developments
P.O. Box 2151
Oxnard, CA 93034

29 Palms California Area Group
c/o Sgt. Wesley Isgrigg
74055 Casita Dr.
29 Palms, CA 92277

UCLA Computer Club
3514 Boelter Hall
Los Angeles, CA 90024

Valley Chapter, SCCS
c/o R. Stuart Gibbs
5652 Lemona Ave.
Van Nuys, CA 91411

Ventura County Computer Society
P.O. Box 525
Port Hueneme, CA 93041

COLORADO

Denver Amateur Computer Society
Jim Clark
P.O. Box 6338
Denver, CO 80206

CONNECTICUT

Amateur Computer Society
Stephen B. Gray
260 Noroton Ave.
Darien, CT 06820

Connecticut Microists
c/o George Ahmuty
6011 Wendy Lane
Westport, CT 06881

Connecticut SCCS
c/o Charles Floto
267 Willow St.
New Haven, CT 06511

University of Hartford
Microcomputer Club
College of Engineering
Dana Hall
200 Bloomfield Ave.
West Hartford, CT 06117

DISTRICT OF COLUMBIA

Washington Amateur Computer
    Society
Robert Jones
4201 Massachusetts Ave.
Apt. 168W
Washington, DC 20016

FLORIDA

Fort Lauderdale Computer Club
c/o Robert Denis
11080 Northwest 39th St.
Coral Springs, FL 33065

Jacksonville Computer Club
Regency East Office Park
9951 Atlantic Blvd., Suite 326
Jacksonville, FL 32211

Miami Area Computer Club
c/o Terry Williamson
P.O. Box 430852, S.
Miami, FL 33143

Miami Computer Club
John Lynn
13431 Southwest 79th St.
Miami, FL 33183

Microcomputer Society of
    Florida
P.O. Box 3284 Downtown Station
Tampa, FL 33604

South Florida Computer Group
410 Northwest 117th St.
Miami, FL 33168

Southern Florida Computer Group
c/o Roberto Denis
11080 Northwest 39th St.
Coral Springs, FL 33065

Space Coast Microcomputer Club
c/o Ray O. Lockwood
1825 Canal Ct.
Merritt Island, FL 32952

Tallahassee Amateur
    Computer Society
Larry Hughes
Route 14, Box 351-116
Tallahassee, FL 32304

University of Florida Amateur
    Computer Society
EE Dept., Room 234
Larsen Hall
Gainesville, FL 32611

GEORGIA

Atlanta Area Microcomputer Club
c/o Jim Dunion
421 Ridgecrest Road
Atlanta, GA 30307

Atlanta Area Microcomputer
    Hobbyist Group
Box 33140
Atlanta, GA 30332

HAWAII

Aloha Computer Club
c/o Robert Kennedy
1541 Dominus, No. 1404
Honolulu, HI 96822

ILLINOIS

Altair-Chicago
517 Talcott Rd.
Park Ridge, IL 60068

Chicago Area Computer Hobbyists
    Exchange (CACHE)
P.O. Box 36
Vernon Hills, IL 60061

Chicago Area Microcomputer Users
    Group
Bill Precht
1102 South Edison
Lombard, IL 60148

Chicago Users Group
195 Ivy Lane
Highland Park, IL 60035

Ice-Nine, Inc.
P.O. Box 291
Western Springs, IL 60558

Indian Hill Computer Club
P. E. Sluka
c/o Bell Telephone Labs
Room 6N227
Naperville, IL 60540

Microcomputer APL Enthusiasts
P.O. Box 574 NUMS
303 East Chicago Ave.
Chicago, IL 60611

No Name Club
c/o Jim Henley
420 Bancroft Ct., No. 8
Rockford, IL 51107

Quand City Computer Club
4211 ½ 7th St.
Rock Island, IL 61201

INDIANA

Beta Iota Tau
Richard R. Petke
RHIT Box 420
Terre Haute, IN 47803

Bloomington Association for
    the Computer Sciences
c/o Remy M. Simpson
901 East 13th St.
Bloomington, IN 47401

Floyd County Computer Enthusiasts
RR2 P.O. Box 466A
New Albany, IN 47150

Hoosier Amateur Computer and
    Kluge Society
c/o Ray Borill
111 South College Ave.
Bloomington, IN 47401

Indiana Small Systems Group
54 Sherry Lane
Brownsburg, IN 46112

Louisville Area Users
   of Microprocessors
115 Edgemont Dr.
New Albany, IN 47150

Purdue University
Computer Hobby Club
Room 67, EE Building
Purdue University
West Lafayette, IN 47907

IOWA

Eastern Iowa Computer Club
6026 Underwood Ave. SW
Cedar Rapids, IA 52404

KANSAS

Computer Network of Kansas City
968 Kansas Ave.
Kansas City, KS 66105

South Central Kansas Amateur
   Computer Association
c/o Cris Borger
1504 North St. Clair
Wichita, KS 67203

KENTUCKY

Louisville Area Users of Computers
P.O. Box 18065
Louisville, KY 40218

LOUISIANA

Dubach Computer Club
Rt. 3, Box 110
Dubach, LA 71235

New Orleans Computer Club
119 Pennsylvania Ave.
Slidell, LA 70458

Tuad City Computer Club
Charles C. Fretwell
2155 West 30th St.
Davenport, LA 52804

MARYLAND

Baltimore Chapter, C.M.C.
Phil Sticha
(301) 682-6000 ex. 304

Chesapeake Microcomputer Club
236 St. David Ct., X4
Cockeysville, MD 21030

Science Education Extension
John David Garcia
11516 LeHavre Dr.
Potomac, Maryland 20854

MASSACHUSETTS

Alcove Computer Club
John P. Vullo
21 Sunset Ave.
North Reading, MA 01864

Greater Boston
   Computer Users Group
Steven Hain
40 Wilshire Dr., Door 2
Sharon, MA 02067

New England Computer Society
P.O. Box 198
Bedford, MA 01730

MICHIGAN

Ann Arbor Computing Club
Roger Gregory
1458 New Port Rd.
Ann Arbor, MI 48103

Computer Hobbyists
    Around Lansing
Joyce and Marvin Church
4307 Mar Moor Dr.
Lansing, MI 48917

Detroit Area Club
Dennis Siemit
45466 Cluster
Utica, MI 48087

Detroit Area Users Group
Dana Badertscher
18300 Ash
East Detroit, MI 48021

Jackson Hams & Hackers
    Commonwealth Association
209 East Washington St.
Jackson, MI 49201

Mid-Michigan Computer Club
15151 Ripple Dr.
Linden, MI 48451

Mid-Michigan Micro Group
William Serviss
13121 Tucker St.
DeWitt, MI 48820

SEMCO
Dick Weir
20,000 Great Oak Circle South
Mt. Clemens, MI 48043

MINNESOTA

Bit Users Association
Resource Access Center
3010 Fourth Ave. South
Minneapolis, MN 55408

Minnesota Computer Society
P.O. Box 35317
Minneapolis, MN 55435

SCEAM Resource Access Center
c/o Richard Koplow
3010 Fourth Ave. South
Minneapolis, MN 55408

Southern Minnesota Amateur
    Computer Club
2212 Northwest 17th Ave.
Rochester, MN 55901

XXX-11 Users Group
Dick Corner
514 South 9th St.
Moorhead, MN 56560

MISSOURI

St. Louis Area Computer Club
Lou Elkins
P.O. Box 1143
St. Louis, MO 63188

MONTANA

Flathead Computer Society
Ernest G. Brooner
P.O. Box 236
Lakeside, MT 59922

NEVADA

Northern Nevada Amateur
    Computer Club
P.O. Box 9068
Reno, NV 89507

NEW HAMPSHIRE

Nashua Area Computer Club
Dwayne Jeffries
181 Cypress Lane
Nashua, NH 03060

New England Computer Club
70 Main St.
Peterborough, NH 03458

NEW JERSEY

Amateur Computer
    Group of New Jersey
c/o Sol Libes
UCTI
1776 Raritan Road
Scotch Plains, NJ 07076

Holmdel Microprocessor Club
c/o Fred Horney
Rm. 3D317
Bell Telephone Labs
Holmdel, NJ 07733

New Jersey Club
Bruce C. Dalland
37 Brook Dr.
Dover, NJ 07801

Northern New Jersey
    Amateur Computer Group
c/o Murray P. Dwight
593 New York Ave.
Lyndhurst, NJ 07071

NEW MEXICO

Albuquerque Area Computer Club
Gary Tack
P.O. Box 866
Corrales, NM 87048

US Robotics Society
P.O. Box 26484
Albuquerque NM 87125

NEW YORK

Buffalo Club
c/o Chuck Fischer
355 South Creek Dr.
Depew, NY 14043

Ithaca Computer Club
Steven Edelman
204 Dryden Rd.
Ithaca, NY 14850

Long Island Computer
    Association
c/o Gary Harrison
P.O. Box 864
Jamaica, NY 11431

Long Island Computer Club
c/o Popular Electronics
One Park Ave.
New York, NY 10016

New York Amateur Computer Club
106 Bedford St.
New York, NY 10014

New York Micro Hobbyists Group
c/o Robert Schwartz
375 Riverside Dr., Apt. 1E
New York, NY 10025

Niagara Region Computer Club
c/o Chuck Fischer
355 South Creek Dr.
Depew, NY 14043

Pacesetter User's Group
1457 Broadway, Rm. 305
New York, NY 10016

RAMS
P.O. Box D
Rochester, NY 14609

Stony Brook Home-Brew
    Computer Club
c/o Ludwig Braun
College of Engineering
    and Applied Sciences
State University of NY
    at Stony Brook
Stony Brook, NY 11794

Students Cybernetics Lab
16 Linwood Ave.
Buffalo, NY 14209

Westchester Amateur Computer
    Society
c/o Harold Shair
41 Colby Ave.
Rye, NY 10580

Westchester Fairfield Amateur
    Computer Society
RR1, Box 198
Pound Ridge, NY 10576

NORTH CAROLINA

Triad Amateur Computer Society
Doug Drye
3202 Winchester Dr.
Greensboro, NC 27406

Triangle Amateur Computer Club
P.O. Box 17523
Raleigh, NC 27609

OHIO

Amateur Computer Society
    of Columbus
c/o Walter Marvin
408 Thurber Dr. West, No. 6
Columbus, OH 43216

Cleveland Digital Group
John Kabat, Jr.
1200 Seneca Blvd., #407
Broadway Heights, OH 44147

Compute, Evaluate, Trade
P.O. Box 104
Tipp City, OH 45371

Dayton Computer Club
Doug Andrew
8668 Sturbridge Ave.
Cincinnati, OH 45200

KIM Users Group
Eric Rehnke
7656 Broadview Rd., Apt. 207
Parma, OH 44134

Midwest Alliance of
    Computer Clubs
Gary Coleman
P.O. Box 83
Brecksville, OH 44141

Universe Unlimited Group
11981 Forest Ave.
Cleveland, OH 44120

OKLAHOMA

Central Oklahoma Amateur
    Computing Society
Lee Lilly
P.O. Box 2213
Norman, OK 73069

Oklahoma City Club
Bill Cowden
2412 SW 45th
Oklahoma City, OK 73110

Tulsa Computer Society
P.O. Box 1133
Tulsa, OK 74101

OREGON

Portland Computer Club
Bill Marsh
2814 Northeast 40th St.
Portland, OR 97212

Portland Computer Society
1003 Garland St., Apt. 4
Woodburn, OR 97071

PENNSYLVANIA

Delaware Valley Chapter, SCCS
Martin Dimmerman
1228 Barrowdale
Rydal, PA 19046

Northeast Computer Association
834 Lawler St.
Philadelphia, PA 19116

OPUS-1
Fred Kitman
400 Smithfield Rd.
Pittsburgh, PA 15222

Philadelphia Area Computer Society
P.O. Box 1954
Philadelphia, PA 19105

Philadelphia Area Club
404 Quince St.
Philadelphia, PA 19147

St. Thomas District HS Computer
Club
1025 Braddock Ave.
Braddock, PA 15104

Wilkes College Computer Club
Erick Jansen, Math Dept.
Wilkes College
Wilkes-Barre, PA 18703

RHODE ISLAND

R.I. Computer Hobbyist Club
16 Grinnell St.
Jamestown, RI 02834

TEXAS

Central Texas
    Computer Association
c/o Ray McCoy
508 Blueberry Hill
Austin, TX 78745

Computer Hobby Group of North
    Texas
Bill Fuller
2377 Dalworth, #157
Grand Prairie, TX 75050

El Paso Computer Group
Jack O. Coats, Jr.
213 Argonaut, Apt. 27
El Paso, TX 79912

Houston Amateur Computer Club
Steve Smith
3842 Grennock
Houston, TX 77025

Microcomputer Tinkers & Co.
William Peters
3845 Le Bleu
Beaumont, TX 77707

NASA-JSC Computer Hobbyist Club
Marlowe Cassetti
1011 Davenport
Seabrook, TX 77586

Northside Computer Group
2318 Town Breeze
San Antonio, TX 78238

Panhandle Computer Society
Tex Everett
2923 Spring
Amarillo, TX 79103

Permian Basin Computer Group
John Rabenaldt
Ector County School District
P.O. Box 3912
Odessa, TX 79760

San Antonio Computer Club
7517 Jonquil
San Antonio, TX 78233

South Texas Computer Club
11246 S. Post Oak Rd.
Suite 125
Houston, TX 77035

Texas A&M University
    Microcomputer
Box M-9
Aggieland Station, TX 77844

Texas Computer Club
L. G. Walker
Route 1, Box 272
Aledo, TX 76008

UTAH

Salt Lake City Computer Club
1928 South 2600 East
Salt Lake City, UT 84108

VIRGINIA

Alexandria Chapter, CMC
Richard Rubinstein
7711 Elba Rd.
Alexandria, VA 22306

AMRAD
1524 Springville Ave.
McLean, VA 22101

Charlottesville Computer
    Hobbyist Club
P.O. Box 6132
Charlottesville, VA 22906

Dyna-Micro Users Group
Dr. Frank Settle, Jr.
Digital Directions
P.O. Box 1053
Lexington, VA 24450

IBM 5100 Users Group
Richard E. Easton, MD
5541 Parliment Dr., Suite 104
Virginia Beach, VA 23462

McLean Chapter, CMC
Carlyle Reader
(703) 471-5600

Peninsula Computer Hobbyist Club
Larry Polis
2 Weber Lane
Hampton, VA 23663

Reston Chapter, CMC
Andrew Convery
2315 Freetown Cr., Apt. 110
Reston, VA 22091

Richmond Chapter, CMC
Hugh Melton
(804) 285-2452

Roanoke Valley Computer Club
Lee Yosafat
2026 Wynmere Dr. SW
Roanoke, VA 24018

WASHINGTON

Northwest Computer Club
P.O. Box 5304
Drsyylr, ES

Northwest Computer Club
P.O. Box 5304
Seattle, WA 98105

WISCONSIN

Durant Club
James S. White
901 South 12th St.
Watertown, WI 53094

Wisconsin Area Tribe of Computer
    Hobbyists (WATCH)
Don Stevens
P.O. Box 159
Sheboygan Falls, WI 53085

CANADA

Amateur Microprocessor
    Club of Kitchner-Waterloo
Ed Spike
Electrical Engineering Dept.
University of Waterloo
Waterloo, Ontario N2L 3Gl

Canadian Computer Club
861 111th St.
Brandon, Manitoba R7A 4L1

Montreal Area Computer Society
Leslie Zoltan
4100 Kindersley Ave., Apt. 22
Montreal, Quebec

Montreal Micro-68 Computer Club
Case Postale at Succor Sale
Montreal, Canada H4Y 1A2

Ottawa Computer Group
Box 13218
Kanata, Ontario, K2A 1X4

Societe d'Informatique Amateur du
    Quebec
376 du Roi, Suite 304
Quebec, Canada PQ 2W6

Toronto Region of Computer
    Enthusiasts (TRACE)
Harold G. Melanson
Box 545
Streetsville, Ontario L5M 2C1

FOREIGN

Amateur Computer Club
7 Dordells
Basildon, Essex, England

Personal Computing Club
c/o The Micro-B Computer Store
22 Lemon Street
Truro, Cornwall England, TR1 2L5

GLOSSARY

Accumulator   The part of the Arithmetic/Logic Unit (ALU) of a computer where binary numbers are added.

Applications   Term applies to what computers are used for. A computer application is a job that the computer does.

Application software   Programs written for the computer to solve specific problems.

Arithmetic/Logic Unit (ALU)   That part of the Central Processing Unit (CPU) where binary data is acted upon. The accumulator is part of the ALU.

Binary number   A number based on two digits, 0 and 1. Binary numbers are used in computers because an electric current can be either on or off.

BASIC   An acronym for Beginners All-purpose Symbolic Instruction Code. This programming language is one of the simplest programming languages and is used on many personal computers.

Bit   The basic unit of data used by computers. A bit is a binary number. It can be either a 1 or a 0.

Byte   A unit of information in computers. Typically with personal computers, a byte is eight bits. On larger computers, a byte may be twelve, or sixteen or more bits.

Chip   Slang for Integrated Circuit (IC). See Integrated Circuit for further definition.

COBOL   An acronym for Common Business-Oriented Language. A programming language used widely by businesses.

Complementary arithmetic   A math technique used by computers whereby numbers can be subtracted or divided through addition.

Computer system   A computer system consists of the computer and all related hardware. A typical system might include a computer, a floppy disk, a video terminal, and a line printer.

Control unit   The internal part of a computer that directs binary data in and out of the computer and to other internal parts.

Core memory   The internal memory of a computer. Originally, this memory consisted of magnetic cores made of tiny rings of magnetic material strung on a grid of fine wire. Today, internal memory consists of integrated circuits (ICs).

Central Processing Unit (CPU)   The brains of the computer, where binary data is manipulated. In personal computers, the CPU is contained on one integrated circuit (IC) called a microprocessor.

Cursor   An indicator (usually a star or an asterisk) on a video display terminal that indicates a character that must be corrected or a position where data is to be entered.

Daisy wheel   A circular print mechanism used in some line printers for impact printing.

Data   A general term referring to any or all facts, numbers, letters, and symbols which can be processed or used by a computer.

Disk BASIC   A BASIC language with specific commands and statements for use with a disc storage unit.

Disk controller   That part of a disk storage unit which controls the interaction between the disk and the computer.

Disk drive   The main unit in a disk storage system. A floppy or a hard disk fits into this unit. Information is either read from the disk or written on it.

Disk Operating System (DOS)   The software needed to make a disk storage unit function with a computer.

External memory   Memory used by the computer for storing information or programs that are not inside the computer. External memory is usually stored on cassette tape, floppy or hard disk, or on paper tape.

Firmware   A combination of hardware and software. Usually refers to software that is stored permanently on Read Only Memory chips (ROM).

Floppy disk   A storage device made of thin, flexible material that is somewhat similar to a record, except that it is square. A full-sized floppy disk will typically store 250,000 bytes of information.

FORTRAN   An acronym for FORmula TRANslator. FORTRAN is the most widely used scientific programming language. It is taught in many universities throughout the world.

Hardware   The physical devices that form a computer system—as opposed to software, which is the instructions for running a computer system. Hardware includes all mechanical, magnetic, electronic, electromechanical, and electric devices found in a computer system.

High-level language   Software that makes it possible to program a computer in English-type statements and commands. BASIC, COBOL, and FORTRAN are all examples.

Input   Refers to the data that is put into the computer.

Integrated Circuit (IC)   A solid state device containing many hundreds of circuits on a single chip of silicon. Also refered to as a chip.

Interactive computing   Computing where the computer responds almost immediately to the input of the user. The interactive nature of personal computers makes them particularly valuable for educational applications.

Internal memory   Computer memory which is located inside the computer itself.

Interface   To connect one computer device to another. When a line printer is connected to a computer it is interfaced to the computer.

Machine language   The basic instructions that a computer can carry out. High-level language instructions are broken down into machine language instructions by the computer before they are acted upon.

Maxicomputers   Large computers used primarily by large institutions.

Microcomputers   Small computers whose central processing units (CPUs) are contained on one single integrated circuit called a microprocessor.

Microprocessor   An integrated circuit (IC) that contains the complete central processing unit (CPU) for a computer. The most common microprocessor chips used in personal computers are the 8080, 6800, Z-80, and 6502.

Minicomputers   Medium-sized computers used by many schools and businesses.

Monitor   Software for handling the input and output of data between the computer and peripheral devices such as cassette tape recorders, line printers, and video monitors.

Nonvolatile   This term is used to refer to memory which is semi-permanent. That is, the memory is not lost when there is no current present. Memory stored on cassette tapes, floppy disks, and paper tape is nonvolatile.

Operating system   An enlarged version of a monitor. Used to control all the operations between a computer and its peripheral devices.

Output   Information which comes out of a computer.

Peripheral   Any external device that can be connected or interfaced to a computer. Line printers, video monitors, and disk drives are examples of peripherals.

Personal computers   Computers which are inexpensive enough and simple enough to be owned by and used by average individuals.

Program   A series of instructions to a computer telling it how to solve a particular problem.

Programmable Read Only Memory (PROM)   Nonvolatile memory stored on an integrated circuit from which the computer can read information but on which information cannot be stored. It is programmable because the information on it can be changed by a device called a PROM programmer.

Read Only Memory (ROM)   Permanent, nonvolatile memory stored on an integrated circuit (IC). Typically, the BASIC language used by many personal computers is stored on ROM.

Random Access Memory (RAM)   The volatile, internal-working memory of a computer that is stored on integrated circuits. It is called random access because the computer can read memory stored on the chips or write new memory onto the chips.

RS232   The standard interface circuitry found on computers.

Sequential memory   Memory that is stored in sequence; that is, programs and data that are stored one after another as with memory stored on cassette tapes. Access to sequential memory is much slower than access to nonsequential memory such as the memory stored on a floppy disk.

Software   Refers to all the instructions used by a computer to perform any function. Includes languages, monitors, operating systems, programs, and application programs.

INDEX